D0429405

The Letters That Hollywood Loved

One Woman's Messages of Christmas and Love That Touched Hearts Around the World

The Letters That Hollywood Loved

One Woman's Messages of Christmas and Love That Touched Hearts Around the World

Lorraine Williams

Foreword by Elmo Williams

Edited by Heidi Ratner-Connolly

Dedication

To Stacy Williams and Jody Jessick, my two lovely and loving daughters, my son, Toby Williams, and Elmo, my husband of 64 years.

Foreword

Lorraine Bennet Cunningham Williams was born in Portland, Oregon on January 28, 1919. Lorraine's mother, Nina, was a beautiful woman. She was unsuccessful in her first three marriages, but on the fourth try she would marry the man that was to be with her the rest of her life.

Lorraine had a closer relationship with her grandmother than she did with her own mother. Lorraine called her "Moremamma". From her, Lorraine learned to observe and love nature. Moremamma taught her the magic of expressing herself with words. At eventide, the two of them sipped tea and read poetry while watching the fading day.

Nina left Portland when Lorraine was three to take up residence in a small apartment in Long Beach, California. When Lorraine was four, her mother married a good-natured Irishman named Floyd Cunningham. Floyd adopted Lorraine and as long as he lived he and Lorraine enjoyed a wonderful companionship. He was the only father she ever talked about. When she finished her high school in Long Beach, Floyd paid tuition at Immaculate Heart College because Lorraine wanted to study classical music. She had a remarkable singing voice, coached and trained in the classics by Madame Elfreda Wynn, Nelson Eddy's teacher.

Lorraine was a grade A student all her life. During her four years in college, she had the major singing role in the many operettas staged at the college. Although she was the only Protestant in the otherwise Catholic university, the nuns adopted and praised her for her dedication to learning, for her willingness to volunteer for extracurricular activities, and for her beautiful singing voice. Lorraine's affection for the nuns always occupied a special place in her heart.

I met Lorraine just as she was starting her senior year in college. We enjoyed each other's company from the beginning. She could always find me in the front row when she was singing. She loved peonies so she always had a bouquet of them waiting for her at the end of her performance. When RKO sent me to New York to finalize the cut on a film, I knew I did not want to lose her. I rushed out, bought an engagement ring, met Lorraine on a tree-lined street in Beverly Hills, gave her the ring and, with a quick kiss, sealed a promise to wed.

On the twenty-third of December, 1940, we exchanged vows at the Little Church of the Flowers in Glendale. We would be husband and wife for sixty-four glorious years. She gave up an opportunity to sing with the San Francisco Opera Company to be a housewife. As I pursued my career in motion pictures, Lorraine followed me to Mexico, to France, to England, and to Germany when my work took me there. Along the way, we found it in our hearts to adopt three remarkable children. Lorraine had the enormous task of raising them while coping with the restrictions of foreign languages and customs that were so different from her own. No matter where we were, she always made a wonderful home for us. We were her happy and grateful family.

During the more than six decades we traveled together, Lorraine gathered material for the letters she sent home expressing her observations and perspective of everything she experienced, so that her friends and family could share her adventures and her joy for living. Her numberous letters to America documented our life's adventures in lyrical and funny language. Her ability to touch both your funnybone and your heart is astonishing. This collection of letters, then, reflects one woman's journey through a life lived with gusto and boundless love for all of us.

Although her letters documented our daily lives, Lorraine always set aside time at the Christmas season to express the gratitude she felt for the privilege of life. Her letters through the years had a way of touching all our hearts—they were collected, treasured, read, and re-read. I loved her for all that she shared, for all that she was, and for her abundant love for everyone.

I have found that in reading these letters at times a little extra information is required to keep our readers oriented as to time and place, so now and then I'll be speaking to you myself to provide those clues.

Here, then, is a collection of her letters that I am privileged to share with every on of you.

Elmo Williams, 2005

California

Lorraine Williams

Pacific Palisades, California, 1952

Musings

Dear Ones,

Some times are just "sometimes". Others are fragments of eternity, tiny shards of joy, poignant and precious. It is a handful of these that, gratefully, I give to you today. These are the "once-upon-a times".

Once upon a time I hurried down a traffic-clotted street where shabby buildings shouldered up a sagging fence drunk with the green glory of ivy. It begged for me to stop just for a glance, but instead I gave—and got—time. Standing there I saw the ivy vines of ancient Greece with sandal prints of philosophers still warm in the path. Stonehenge was there with winter breathing white mists through the plinths. I smelled all the rainforests of all the north, heard voices of Italian fountains, and touched, for an instant, all the uncounted human hands that had ever made small pockets in the coat of earth so that ivy could grow and reach out in supplication. Then, in all that green growing I was given a treasure, a mutation of tendrils being smothered by a parasite vine, the stems fighting valiantly to be what they were meant to be against smothering twists wrapping around them. The struggle had made them unspeakably beautiful with striations of gold and gunmetal and ruby red with edges of ruffled copper. These branches I broke free, unwound the constricting bands, and brought home with me. Now there is a bowl of forever in my kitchen.

Once upon a time a squirrel in our sycamore tree called me to stand, humbled, on the ground while he preached at me, and I learned what wind said and sky felt and that a teacher must never grow too old to be taught.

Once upon a time our turtle laboriously clutched her way up onto the big rock that was her island in the fish pond. One by one she stretched her legs with their preposterous webbed feet and arched her armored neck until she was shaped like a living bowl to catch the sun. Then she turned her head and winked at me to share that exultant moment every dancer feels at the top of his leap, that every wave knows at its cresting.

Once upon a time a stranger smiled at me, answering my inside smile, and two books were written with a single glance. Once upon a time a golden rose fell apart in my hand and made me realize how foolish it is to want the sun when we can own a rose, or an egg, for one mystery is equal to the other. Once upon a time Bach's music and I shouted out loud in unison, "Oh yes, God!" Once upon a time I brought the tiniest snail in the world in with flowers from the garden and, when he discovered me, he stuck his neck out and wagged his antennae in such indignation that I apologized and carried him back out on a leaf.

And once upon a time I was an empty house slamming doors shut to one room after another, closing out the people who had hurt me so. But, when I reached the last room, I was not alone. There, with me, were all of you waiting. Despair could not close in on me for your faith in me was like a small candle writing in the darkness, "To be invincible, you must also be vulnerable."

Today is Thanksgiving Day and I give thanks for so much and so many. For the privilege of life, for those who led me as a child, for the children who have let me lead them, and for Elmo who has held my hand along the way.

I give thanks, too, for laughter that loosens the tight threads of necessity, for sadness that drains away what is unimportant, for fear that shakes away vanity, for sky and earth and all growing things that nourish our souls, and for all the "once-upon-a-times".

Love,
Lorraine

Lorraine Williams

Hollywood, California, 1953

To Be Thanks-giving

Dear Ones,

Tomorrow is Thanksgiving—or is it? Well, at least it is a celebration our history books tell us began almost concurrent with the beginning of this nation of ours. But, then, sometimes the history books are wrong. I think no one, perhaps, really knows precisely when the first Thanksgiving was.

Tradition tells us the Pilgrims set aside a day of prayer and feasting to denote a year's survival in this new and frightening land. But if we look deeper into the matter we will find that each of the colonies had set aside such a day. It was not a new tradition but an old one that the first European settlers had brought with them from the old countries.

Throughout the world—throughout all recorded history—men have rejoiced at the time of harvest, when crops planted in the cold misting days of springtime or in the searing days of summer survived and flourished and were bountiful enough to feed and sustain those who tended them until the next harvesting. According to their concepts and knowledge of earth and sun and rain and whatever gods they believed had blessed them, people paid homage.

But, even before that, did not some truly primitive man feel a surge of gratitude when he found a bee tree and was able to take honey home to children who had never known sweetness? Did not some primitive women, whose brood was winter-starving, come across a cache of frozen meat in some dark forgotten cave and cry with joy?

This day goes a long way back—much farther than we shall ever know—or even imagine. It is imbedded into the instincts that sleep within each of us. Today we have the symbols, the trappings, but have we forgotten what they mean? That this is the "pausing time" in the cycle of the year, the time to gather in and then pour forth all that we have worked for. "As we have planted, so have we reaped."

Yet, are we not part of the harvest of this earth, of generations before us? Did not each of us grow according to our inheritance, according to our environment, according to our time? Are we not different, each from the other—from every other human being on this earth? And yet we have a special difference! For we are the only creatures on this earth that can set outside of ourselves and examine our lives, who can look back and look ahead, the only ones who can laugh—or cry—and know why. And we are the only creatures who have the capacity to change!

So, on Thanksgiving let's open the storehouse of ourselves. There will be a lot to examine, to weigh, to evaluate. First off: the privilege of life itself. The "*I'm here*!" in a meaningful place among my own kind. I have family and friends, talents, skills, intelligence, health, vitality, work to do and the rewards it brings. I am alive in one of the best places of the world in one of the best times of the world. For I am free to choose from many choices. I am free to change the things I dislike in my life, and free to enjoy the things I like.

I need not strive for impossible perfection but, instead, can seek for whatever is best, whatever is unique, in me. I need not be bitter about my shortcomings for I can overcome them. Instead I will recognize all my good qualities, all my accomplishments, all my potentials. And when I count them all up, I will be filled with thanks for who I am, what I am, that I am...

For it is only when I am THANK-FULL that I can truly know what it is to be THANKS-GIVING.

Love,
Lorraine

England

1954 was one of those years that are hard to categorize; It held great promise but turned out to be something else. I had signed to direct a film that would star Jan Sterling, Paul Douglas, Dirk Bogard and Diana Doors. Financing for the film fell apart; so did my cast. When it was all over, I had made a cult film – voted as the worst film of the decade. But nothing is all bad, it seems. The assignment afforded me the opportunity to take Lorraine to London for her first visit. Although I had lived there from 1933 until 1938, it was wonderful to get a fresh look at the old city through Lorraine's eyes.

– Elmo

Lorraine Williams

The Dorchester Hotel, London, December, 1954

Good Morning,

Well, so far, London has really been good to us! The weather has been unbelievably good and the sun actually broke through for about ten minutes this morning. For a city where it is still dark at eight o'clock in the morning and dark again by four in the afternoon, sunshine is a rarity, believe me! The operators in the "lifts" (elevators), the tail-coated waiters, the scurrying housemaids and charwomen, and all the various and sundry staff are quite proud of their unusual weather and their grins and comments are as bright as the sky was for a few moments. But in the main the British are still skeptics; they keep their umbrellas with them, and I do too, although I haven't had much use for mine yet except to stumble over, leave in the taxi (and only rescue at the last possible moment), and drop at least three times in each walk. For we have been walking a great deal and only have taken a taxi or bus on a few occasions when we got so far away from the hotel that my ankles began to wobble. The air is so brisk and the mood of the city so captivating that Elmo and I cover miles and miles afoot. There is always something new and interesting to see or smell or listen to just a bit up ahead.

The Dorchester is one of the swankier hotels in the smart West End of London. As much as we are enjoying the ultimate in luxury, we hope to find a "flat" (apartment) soon, so today the estate agent, Mr. Mayor, has promised to take us 'round looking. We have been primed by our American friends to insist upon one that has (1) central heating, (2) continuous hot water, (3) porterage, and (4) a telephone. I have been warned not to fall for the atmosphere no matter how quaintly Victorian or how accessible the location unless these qualifications are met. The Dorchester has *not* been typical of average conditions, I gather. In fact they are so determined to please us that we have had difficulty getting the temperatures below ninety in our room. There is a lever to control the heat (pronounced, of course, lee-vah!) and we keep pushing it to the cold side but still the heat wells and bubbles up through the register. They have provided the beds with at least forty-five pounds of coverings. The heavy comforter and two blankets at least an inch thick are guaranteed to make an Eskimo sweat, two enormous and unyielding pillows, plus a woolen throw in case your feet get cold and a coverlet as stiff and heavy as a Turkish carpet are all, I think, almost enough to keep even a thin-blooded Californian warm.

Our bathroom is a delight. Overall dimensions are about 10 x 18 feet and the ceiling is at least 12 or 14 feet high. The bathtub is both broad and long enough to drown an elephant while its progeny could be safely laundered in the basin. The toilet ("water closet", *please*) is quite ordinary except for the elaborate piping system that snakes along over two walls and a cleverly concealed flushing device. The first time I engaged in a coy search for said handle—above, below, and then behind the appliance—I mistakenly pulled the chain that opened the traverse draperies at the window. Finally, though, I spied a faceplate with a bronze handle that could be turned or cranked around. It works fine except each time I use it I feel like I'm turning on the current for an electrocution!

Our bath is tiled with Dutch Delphtian tiles. Spaced every now and then is a scenic blue and white one depicting some sort of quaint activity on a miniscule island. My favorite one shows a boy and girl engaged in a touching scene. Directly over the tub and well within reach of the bather are two buttons—one to summon the valet, the green button, and one to summon the maid, the red button, and right next to the buttons on a hook is a bat! That is, I thought it was a bat since it is half the size of a tennis racket and solid sturdy oak. In my ignorance I thought it was to defend oneself if you accidentally got the wrong gender of back-scrubber but I find, on turning it over, that it is a floating thermometer. The scale ranges from 40 degrees Fahrenheit (which they designate as "cool") to 120 degrees which the Dorchester no doubt considers hot enough for any American. But, dearest to my heart is the bath ("bawth") chair! Beside the tub is a wooden capacious armchair which the maid has draped with an enormous fluffy towel. You step out of the *bawth* and sit down in the chair, envelop yourself in towel and meditate as you dry. This is it, kids, and next to a title I think the *bawth*chair the ultimate, ultimate in posh living. But here Elmo and I differ. His vote (since he is the stand up and snort-and-see-saw-the-towel-across-your-back type) is for the heated towel rack. I must agree that they are fifty years ahead of us on this. It looks like a jungle-gym of fat chrome pipes through which the hot water runs and upon which repose those enormous carpet-sized towels that, as a result, are always cozy warm. For the drying of our chorus-girl wash each night it is a dream. That way we can get the wash out of the way before the staff discovers us! Incidentally, these same hot water pipes are threaded back and forth under the tile floor so that you have the same sensation walking barefoot as you do crossing the sand dunes of Death Valley on a summer day. It's wonderful!

So far life here has been wonderful indeed except for the inconvenience of not understanding half of what is said, and, for me, having a pocketful of strange and confused money. But the people are remarkably patient, having dealt with many odd Americans. I'm sure they think we are either (1) filthy rich and utterly spoiled or (2) gangsters. In either respect they find it advisable to cater to you. Their traffic is worse than ours—*honestly!* Elmo and I are eternally snatching each other out of the path of two-story busses or hurtling little cars. They only drive with parking lights at night and I feel as if I'm being stalked by the "Black Leopards" that run in packs. There is a hustle and rush and constant sound befitting to the world's largest city. There seems to me to be an exceptional amount of friendliness and quite an open curiosity about us (I think they expect me to swallow the spoon when I drink tea), and as is always true, a smile invites a smile.

The mood of the city has me captive, the green of grass in Hyde Park and Green Park and St. James Park is startling, the trees are black and bare, and the sky is eternal grey in every shade and mutation. Except for today, that is. A glance out the window shows a streak or two of blue and some clouds too high to be smudged by the pervading coal smoke. It looks so appetizing I think I'll get Elmo to join me and go for a walk.

Though London welcomed us, the scars of the bombing by Germany in World War II were still evident in a number of neighborhoods. During our frequent walks, it was our habit to stop for a few minutes beside the devastation left by one of those bombs to guess what life must have been like in that place and at that time.

In this city where steeples are held up by courage
Where crippled clocks look neither backwards nor forwards but into the hearts of men...

Where there are great holes that once were homes
With bombs, the janitor of the ages
Where children fretted in their sleep
At the distant mutter of summer thunder

What can we say—or do—or live?
That can undo what once was done.

Houses were dreams and mortar
Flesh craved only air to breathe
and beds to lie down in

But the children, unborn, unbegotten
Died with their fathers—
snuffed out with pincers of steel.

The blue eyes that never lift
to the drone of dragon fly
The feet that never scuff home
to where there is no home.

The child all mothers' arms ache
to hold will never be.

War is nothing. This is tragedy!

Lorraine

Lorraine Williams

December 23-24, 1954

Top o' the mornin' to ye!

After two days of pampered confinement, my shoelaces were ready for London. The only problem, my dears, was that I could not understand what they were saying—and in my own language yet. Eventually I ventured out and, remembering warnings about traffic coming the wrong direction, looked left, looked right, looked confused, and finally just waited until no one was coming from any direction. Crossing into Hyde Park, the world's biggest front yard, I followed several miles of beckoning paths when, without so much as a by-your-leave, it began to snow. There I was in a Californian coat with Californian blood in Californian veins and my sanctuary, the Dorchester, obliterated in a world the color of skim milk. I floundered on but all sounds of traffic that might lead me out were smothered and there was no sign of human life except once when a phantom bobbie went riding through on a bicycle with his peaked black helmet bent low over the handlebars and his black slicker blowing out behind him. By the time I reached where he had been he was gone, and there was only a huddle of forlorn chairs and a turnstile with no one to go through it but me and a ranging Airedale, who gave me a disbelieving look as he widdled on the post. I tried to follow him but moving into the storm just took my breath away and, when I stopped to catch it, he was gone too.

By now snow had piled up on my head and my eyebrows, filled my coat cuffs and infiltrated into my pockets where my hands were slowly freezing. But as I was starting to wish I'd paid more attention to the symptoms of hypothermia, I suddenly walked directly into a tea kiosk. As I collapsed into the nearest chair and began to thaw, a small, dark-haired waitress came to take my order. I asked for a ham sandwich and a cup of coffee. She brought me a piece of apple pie and a pot of tea. I didn't understand her and she didn't understand me. I would have cried except my tears would have come out sleet! (Months later, another visit to that kiosk and I discovered that she was an émigré from Hungary and just learning the language too. I could have hugged her then.)

An hour later the storm had blown past so I went back out, this time into a black and white etching, the kind I had seen before but never been a part of. The park was great glistening expanses of white studded with black bare-armed trees. Ornate wrought iron fences wore white snowcaps and the gingerbread bandstand was festooned with a filigree of snow lace. The only thing that was not black or white was a pond, gone slate grey with little scallops of ice, like the thinnest porcelain forming around its edges. I passed a lady all bundled up in furs walking her dog. We smiled and I had a commiserating look for that small Skye terrier with legs so short that he had to fling them out like a trotter horse and push his belly through four inches of snow. At last I saw the bulk of the hotel loom up ahead and rejoiced to see that grand oversized doorman heading towards me with his grand oversized umbrella. Reaching out to shelter me could only have been a welcoming gesture for by now no more moisture was coming down from the sky; it was all dripping off of me, the coronet of snow half-melted down the back of my neck and filtered down to shoes where it was squishing out of the open toes. But what consolation there was when I understood his greeting, "Been to Alaska, 'ave ye?" and "'Ad a nice visit, I 'ope!"

No matter how elegant the Dorchester was, we could not afford it for long. We were in London to work and in no financial position to stay longer than it took to find an affordable place to settle. So I took to the want-ads and the varied and very good public transport and came to love those generous but low-key folks who so indirectly make you welcome. One does not have to actually be lost in London. One has only to look lost for passers-by to wheel about and begin unfolding little maps and waving umbrellas in directions one should go.

Of course I quickly learned "brolly" for umbrella and "face flannel" for washcloth and another whole vocabulary of tit-for-tat words. And I was warned never ever to use either "bum" or "bloody", two words, then, that invariably and insistently kept coming to mind. I bit my lip quite a few times but never ever was it allowed to bleed.

Flat hunting took me all over London, but I kept searching for something in the West End—and almost found a place that I liked but then I missed out because I couldn't follow simple directions. The hall porter had said it was on the third floor so I climbed up the three flights of steps. Only in England the third floor is really the second floor because the first floor is the ground floor and the second floor is the first floor which then makes the third floor the second floor. And while I was figuring that all out another woman came along and rented the flat.

Love,
Lorraine

London, England, December 30, 1954

Dear Family,

This morning I went flat hunting again. Looked at four of them here in the swank West End and wouldn't have picked a chicken in any of them. Such *dirt,* and a dull, dismal, drab, sewer-ish feeling. You see, when anything over here is dirty and unkempt it's been dirty and unkempt for centuries! Most of these buildings are two to three hundred years old and they are, believe it or not, the ultimate in fine living here. Outside of six or seven modern hotels like this (built in 1930 and considered spanking new), even the wealthiest people have toilets ("water closets") with the tank up on the ceiling and the hanging chain and knob. People at a party, for instance, have to sort of space out their visits to the "W.C." since it takes about seven minutes for the tank to fill before it can be flushed again. I know—I was trapped in one for a goodly period at Michael and Jo Carrera's house yesterday. I kept pulling the chain and all that happened was a mild aquatic shudder. Not even a shudder, more of a small shrug! Apologetic, I'm sure.

I've done, by necessity, more drinking here in two weeks than I've done at home in two years. Yesterday, for example, was a Boxing Day party. Come by for drinks at 12:00. Elmo was down with a siege of his pet "bug" so I had to do the honors alone and was I ever scared. Must say I managed to understand about a third of the conversation except for the slang and colloquialisms, although along about four o'clock when the boys were into their ninth drinks they did get awfully smushy and I was dead lost. Wish I had the tape recorder over here to give you a vocal rendition of a proper gent saying, as he bears down on you, glass in hand, cigarette in long holder, *"Oh I say, you're Mrs. Elmo, wot? Delightfully smertish frence whilesome, don't you know? Consuble brumney in twertsy? Um?"* Thank heavens for the universal laugh which was my only comeback. I think they must think I'm half sister to a hyena!

Love,
Lorraine

December 31, 1954

New Year's Eve

Hi, You All!

The best of the season and I hope you are planning on one of those super-duper nights together. How we wish we could do a swift fade out-and fast fade-in and be with you tonight. We *shall* be, though, in thoughts and love. So poke the fire for us; belch with utter contentment and know that while you lift your glasses to us we shall lift our thoughts to you.

This is going to be a hectic one. I've heard that absolutely the most frantic place in the world is Trafalgar Square, heart of London, on New Year's Eve. Guess where we will be? Trafalgar Square, heart of London, of course. We had a hotshot idea that to be able to photograph the masses of celebrating people with a hand-held camera would give scope to our film without paying all those extras. You see, we are currently working on story line where our heroine and two other girls escape from prison just after or at Christmastime. The heroine is trying desperately to escape the police just long enough to return to a small hotel on the north coast where she met and fell in love with a man. They were forced to part but promised each other to meet there in three months. So the girl is fighting to keep this rendezvous with the only good man she has ever known. We figure the effect of a frightened, desperate girl caught up in the happy hysterical crowd should have a strong appeal. That's why Me and Mo, Inc. shall be there working with a cameraman, a bobby and a double for the actress. It is going to be murder but I've got on my low heels, warm coat, and have sharpened both elbows!

The crowds were liquored up and boisterous by the time we got there, and it was cold—bitter cold. Brrrrrr! It started New Year's Eve with the thermometer dropping like a rock in a well and the wind blowing off the river. We were out shooting from six until two the next morning. My feet were so numb I could just shuffle and stumble walking home. Seemed like two-thirds of London was determined to crowd into Piccadilly Circus, Leicester (pronounced "Lester") Square or Trafalgar Square, and the other third was trying to get out!

However, I think we got some good atmospheric stuff with a double for our leading girl and an actor we had with us dressed as a bobby. I was very grateful that, besides being a nice chap, he stayed near me and discouraged the gay ruffians who thought it great sport to grab and kiss the ladies. Didn't much care for any arduous acne embraces meself!

I hope you were lucky enough to celebrate by a nice warm fire, and for the coming new year we wish you all that is good.

With love,
Lorraine

January 1st

New Year's Day

And the Top-of-the-Morning!

(Later on...)

It is now 11a.m. and Elmo and I have been out to look at the flat I saw yesterday afternoon. It is in Chesterfield house, a comparatively new and enormous block of flats just a block or so from the hotel. It is right off the famous Curzon Street and only a hop, skip, and jump from Sherpeard's Market. I am in love with the

Market—it has, in its way, as much charm as Farmer's Market and I think I shall enjoy getting acquainted with the shops and stall keepers. (It is also the rendezvous of the best of London's prostitutes and I will have to keep Elmo on a leash. The girls on Park Lane and Piccadilly are reticent in as much as they only accost the men verbally ("Good evening, sir, do you have a light?"), but the ones in the market grab hold of their arm and try to walk them home! This is a great shock to me—there are hundreds of them in this West End alone—and they are beautiful, smartly-dressed girls. Our friend Tony tells me it is one way to make a good living *without* income tax.) I had to wait a few minutes last night while Elmo ran into a pub for cigarettes. *Believe me,* I kept moving and didn't loiter on the street corner. Also you must *never* stand in a doorway if you are a lone woman or smoke on the street. Of course, if some man did accost me with an indecent proposal, I probably shouldn't understand him. Yipes! Maybe that would be worse! No, they can pretty much spot me for an American every time. My clothes (to my way of thinking anyway) are not much different from the better-dressed English women. My walk is somewhat brisker, but in general demeanor I don't think I'm obvious. Still I get more looks. I find myself muttering, *Well look, damn it, look!*

I think Willie, Elmo's older sister, will join us about the 9th of January. Had a note and she and Reid, her husband, have definitely parted, and are effecting a division of property and things, and she seemed quite relieved about it. We will get her a room here at the Dorchester for the night. I've written and asked her to stay a couple of weeks if she can. We feel that a good rest and visit here should be important to her, a break between leaving her old life and starting the new.

Things seem to be rocking along now. I'm over my fright and have braved the stores, the busses, and the markets alone. Good news came by cable today from Lippert's office in Hollywood, congratulating Elmo on his Oscar nomination for his work on *20,000 Leagues Under The Sea.* Our realtor also phoned to say he'd found yet a different flat that he thinks is our cup of tea. Of course we taxied right over, had a good look, reached agreement for a short-term rental, and Elmo signed.

Well, dear family, it is time to stop and get a little work done. Even though we can't touch hands today, the ring of hearts is unbroken and our best wishes are with you all for 1955. May it bring each of you all the good things you deserve!

Love,
Lorraine

January, 1955, Tuesday Afternoon

Dear Family,

If I don't get a letter off to you all now, I don't know when I'll be able to sneak a few minutes away to do it. So, before Elmo and Tony get in from the country where they have gone to hunt locations and confer with the set director at Bray Studio, I'll just snitch the time it takes to thank you one and all for the lovely letters. Yesterday we had Eunice and Axels' amusing Valentine letter, the long one from Snooks and Curly with the Academy nomination enclosure, the letter Willie mailed from New York, and the one from Mom and Pop telling about Pop's trying to start the car from the backseat! So thank you one and all for all the news and cheering from the home front. If I skip around a lot, it's because I'm weary and worn out from whacking away on dialogue, and so cold I have to get up and do a jig every now and then to warm my fingers so they'll hit the right keys. (I also have a pigeon looking at me sadly about three feet away on the ledge outside the window—the pie tin where I put his bread crumbs and suet is empty because the seagulls have swooped in and chased the pigeons away and gobbled it up.) So, chums, you can see I should be forgiven *all* and *any* aberrations that occur.

Love,
Lorraine

January, 1955

Dear Family,

Well, ducks, here we are, all settled in! And I don't mind confessing that most of our waking hours have been spent huddled around the electric heater in the living…oops!…"drawing" room. It is a small two-coil deal but fashioned to resemble a cheery coal fire, the coal effect being achieved by some lumpy paper mache painted black, an orange bulb not quite concealed behind it, with a small paper pinwheel revolving over it to, I presume, create the devastating illusion of the flickering flame. I only wish they had dispensed with the grand manner and provided it with a bit more heat. Wouldn't you know? The flat had been unoccupied for over a month while Lady Cunninghame (note the "e") had it redecorated and thoroughly (so she said) cleaned. We moved in during the severest cold snap of the year and, coming from the overheated luxury of the Dorchester, had small icicles hanging from our noses half the time. We have all drunk so much hot tea we SLOSH! You know, *Slosh*! Once more—*Slosh*!—oh to hell with it!

Willie, Elmo's older sister, has spent so much time sitting on the floor in front of the heater she is beginning to resemble a duck so I just now stopped and dragged out a little footstool so she could type more comfortably. I'm at the opposite end of the room, but not Willie! She refuses to leave the fire. I find a brisk run around the flat every twenty minutes or so restores the circulation although it probably drives the neighbors below crazy (especially with me wearing my four-pound, fur-lined, artic boots! Oh well, there are Americans below us so they are probably doing it too).

Thank heavens I took the flat that was the smallest of all I saw. Naturally the way things go, it also had the most furniture. There is so much and all of it so big you rather get the feeling that it has tiptoed up behind you and is peeking over your shoulder. There is a big Chinese cabinet in the drawing room that keeps leering at me and I half expect it to throw its doors open like a great mouth and come, snorting fire, after me! There are, and I am exceedingly grateful for, three large chests. In them there now repose seventeen oriental throw rugs, six pillows, eleven worn out brushes, brooms, and mops, sixteen tablecloths that wouldn't fit the table, two hideous bathmats (I'd rather climb out on an ice block than step on one of those), two lumpy feather bolsters from off the bed, and a fantastic collection of early Victorian mason jars Lady Cunninghame amusingly refers to as *vahzes*!

The stove looks like a toy—three little burners, a miniature oven, and tinier grill. The refrigerator (*get this!*) is .75 cubic foot, and the pan cupboard is one vast dark hole with the weirdest assortment of decrepit cookware you could assemble. I just boiled some eggs and kept hearing a hissing noise. Investigation proved that what I thought was the sturdiest pan had a lovely leak and was dribbling water all down inside the stove. Every plug and electrical outlet is a different size, different voltage, and different wattage. I can't imagine why every house in London hasn't burned down since threadbare wires run for miles around the baseboards, slither up wardrobe legs, cross the ceiling (where they are blithely painted over) and down to be wrapped a few times around the radiator, connected through an alarming system of converters and finally plugged into an antique table lamp that falls to pieces the first time we turn it on. Life here has been one long case of utter hysteria!

The bathroom is modern. That is, it has fixtures manufactured since the turn of the century, but you almost break your neck stepping out of the tub unless you are aware that the floor is six inches lower than the tub. I've spent hours, actually, standing in some 4 x 6 broom closet waiting for the jolly old water closet to pump up enough water to flush. Damned embarrassing, wot! You pull the chain and it can't even spit. I'm sure it was times and situations like this that gave the British the stamina and endurance to outlast Hitler!

You mustn't take my complaining seriously, you know. It is all meant in fun. There are some lovely things here and as soon as the dear, jolly old radiators get up wind and the walls warm up and the cold snap breaks, it will be jolly good. Meanwhile we are having a gay old time whipping around London on the red double-decker busses, seeing the sights, whipping into teashops to thaw out (*Slosh!*—there, I sneaked up on it) and bundling around the fire drinking tea and coffee and sherry and Bovril at home. Willie and I have our hot water bottles in bed at night. Elmo scorns them but he wears his longhandles under his pajamas and two pair of wool sox and covers up his head! It is exciting and invigorating and there are three kids over here just whooping it up.

Now I have to brave the bathroom. Haven't bathed in two days—dirt is warm, you know—so I shall take the electric heater and the 25 feet of "flex" (extension cord) and race down the hall ("corridor" over here) and pray that no one else in the building has taken a *bawth* in the past hour. In that case, constant hot water becomes constant lukewarm water and I shall go through my ablutions faster than a stripteaser in the artic. (Pretty much the same idea anyway only mine is motivated by desperation only.)

Will write again soon. Now my fingers have stiffened up—you think I'm kidding?—look at all the typing errors above. Remember I'm at the far end of the room away from the fire. Might stop in and soak my feet with the eggs that are boiling or move beside Willie by the fire! Tomorrow will be the last day of her visit. We're going to miss her.

Love for now!
Lorraine

January, 1955

Dear Friends,

Here we go again!

And I shouldn't, really, since the flat is all in bits and pieces and I should be starting supper, and there is my pet pigeon "door knocker" tapping on the window beside me asking for a handout. But with me, writing letters is like the hives—when I itch, I just have to do something about it.

Today was a bright and sunny day, but with a wind that turned you around corners where you didn't mean to go and sent the "teddy-boys" (fashion plates) chasing their curly-brimmed bowlers down the street. Even though I was low on money, I had a whole day to spend and if you'll bear with me, I'll share it with you.

I left the flat about ten this morning and regretted not wearing a heavier coat, but since there was a bus coming I decided to shiver and run for it. I had determined to find St. Christopher Street which I had heard had a lot of quaint little antique shops on it. First, though, I stopped off at Selfridge's Store, that mecca for "Ameddicuns", and a very nice clerk (pronounced "clark") fixed both our Ronson lighters for a mere seven pence and a friendly smile. Then around the corner to Wigmore Street and some window-shopping until it was noon and I was near my favorite Danish restaurant. Luckily I found a table free beside the coal fire and could sit there and toast and watch the passers-by through the many-paned window. It is a delightful place and lunch will cost you at least an hour and dinner two, but well worth the time. I had a bowl of scalding hot beef soup, a Danish schnitzel with browned potatoes, steamed "swede" (pronounced "rutabaga"), and a delectable little dessert called "klattekage", an egg pancake about six inches across, covered with hot orange sauce, slivered almonds, and floated in rich, pour cream. All this with a glass of wine and a cup of reasonably good black coffee came to eight and eleven and with a shilling tip figured out to $1.37 in Ameddicun! Meanwhile I enjoyed watching the other diners, the service was superb, the food delicious, and the atmosphere with red checkered tablecloths, candles flickering in silver holders, an enormous scrubbed wood table covered with pastries and salads, a paneled wall hung with old violins, mandolins, and horns, and a window box abloom with sharp blue Cinerarias—well, I think I got my money's worth.

Then I buttoned up my coat and skittered on up to find St. Christopher. But I lost it someplace between Marylebone Lane and Wimpole Street. London is like that. North runs southwest and east just went around the corner—but no one complains. The same street changes names four times in four miles and I doubt seriously if there is one square (pronounced "block") that *is* square. Most of them manage to have either three or seven sides and you just think you are circling back to where you left off a while ago. It has been rumored that London was laid out by a designer who followed a drunk Roman to his home!

By the time I had followed that Roman a few miles, I gave up and headed back for Marleybone Lane (only it should be "Marylebone"), and the Cordon Bleu Cookery School where I was privileged, after paying eight and six pence, to observe a demonstration on making French gateaux from two to four. Turning into Number

33, I was quite tempted to just stay in the Cordon Bleu restaurant and not go upstairs to the kitchen. Amazing what a lovely effect simple things can create. The room is about twelve feet wide and maybe thirty-five long. The floor is plain waxed wood, the tables are well scrubbed very plain pine, and the chairs are waxed birch of a simple captain's shape. No pictures or ornate décor—just two large mirrors garlanded around with a lei of vegetables, much like those strings of gourds that were so popular in California a few years back. To my inquiring eye and poking finger, I found they truly were real carrots, turnips, ears of corn, and tomatoes that had been heavily impregnated with wax some way. Against the plain buff walls they were lovely. For wall lights, there were just bulbs cleverly shielded by a charming arrangement of copper fluted molds, wicker bread baskets, and wooden spoons. Several high plate shelves held lovely old copper pieces and tureens and mortars and pestles. And on a plain trestle table under the front window were the remnants of a buffet luncheon spread that made me almost regret my stop at the Danish Restaurant. Strange what attraction the simple and good things of life hold for us—or could it be that I just *love* to eat!

Up three flights of stairs to the kitchen on the second floor. (Oh yes—that's right—the first floor is the ground floor, the second floor is the first floor, making the third floor the second floor.) The kitchen looked like a laboratory (pronounced "lab'try") and the effect was heightened by about twenty girls and women in white uniforms earnestly waiting for whatever operation was about to be performed on the plain kitchen table around which they were seated. Naturally, being the only foreigner present, I came in for many a surreptitious glance and much curiosity, and more so after the instructress asked me if I could understand her and I had to reply in my strange Yankee voice. I had a cute little doll of a girl sitting next to me and she was as interested in my handwriting as I was in hers as we both took down the recipes. My writing is pretty bad after twenty years of pounding my good old typewriter here, but hers was a lovely, strong, straight up and down, almost printed script. That's something that never fails to amaze me here: women write with strong dominant calligraphy while men usually have spidery, delicate penmanship. Don't ask me why it is—it just is!

If I could just figure out how to do it, I'd like to bring my little Cordon Bleu cutie home with me (with a little touch here and there she could give those Hollywood girls a run for their money), and imagine having such a good cook in the house. She is just finishing a year's intensive training. Any offers?

Today we observed Gatteau Helvetia and Gatteau Le Rosemarie. I shall be prepared to demonstrate to those interested upon my return. Tomorrow we do Gatteau Pain Complet which comes out looking, I'm told, like a big round loaf of French country bread and Gatteau Fanny. This latter name was the big joke of the day. They simply exploded and the instructress had to pound on the table with a spoon to restore order since, I find, "fanny" has an even naughtier connotation here that it does at home!

By four the two *gateaux* were baked, adorned, and admired and class was dismissed. I decided to take a shortcut through to St. James Street behind Selfridge's which leads into its grocery department on—yep—you guessed it—St. Christopher's Street. Only it isn't a street but merely a footpath about five feet wide and one I've seen a dozen times and always determined, some day, to go down. Well, since the wind was getting brisker (and you can emphasize the first two letters in brisker), and my tummy was ringing the teatime alarm, I decided just to peek into windows for today and "do" the shops tomorrow. I *hope* I can find it again...but maybe they will have moved it again!

Selfridges's saw me loading my nylon shopping bag with some prime Scotch, salmon steaks, a package of frozen spinach, four small and deah-oh-deah tomatoes, and a head of endive (pronounced "chicory") and those wonderful shiny crusted, chewy, shour (sorry, shouldn't have had that wine for lunch), sour-dough rolls). Oh yes—a hurry back for a pound of Chase and Sanborn and some Danish Bleu cheese and some flaky, sharp Cheddar. Then, ducking and dodging through the going-home rush of cars, busses, and taxis, aboard Number 88, and tuppence worth of ride to Lancaster Gate (pronounced "Lak'str") and up into the lift to good old flat seven. Everything was just as I had left it this morning except that one of the arm chairs had rolled into the dining room—they do that when the underground trains shake the house—one lampshade had fallen off, and "door knocker" was sitting forlornly on the window sill to remind me it was teatime for him too.

All of which brings us round-robin to where we started out. I had a lovely day and hope you enjoyed sharing it with me. After all, it's the next best thing to having you here. Tomorrow more of the same—probably won't spend a halfpenny (pronounced "hapny"), but will come home with another thousand worth of memories!

Love,
Lorraine

February, 1955, London

Dear Family,

Enclosed is a brochure from my very favorite eating place, the Ivy. How I wish you could have been with us.

The food, the atmosphere, and a leisurely two hours for lunch have made us wonder how we can go back often and stay longer. Here is what I had to eat, and all of it so delicious that I can't conceive of proper adjectives. First off, a small tumbler of Scotch to warm us up while we ordered, it being freezing cold and blowing up a gale outside. Then a bowl of scalding hot beef broth followed by a salad of tiny, tiny, northern shrimps which were served cold and buttered. With this a plate of thin-sliced, buttered oatmeal bread. Also a pressed glass stein of Flower's Bitter, a very mild and nutty ale. Then the fish course and a fragile but crisp slice of battered sole. For the entrée I had a lamb chop which was enormous but tender and sweet, and broiled just right together with buttered potatoes and fresh green peas. The rolls were either flaky crescents or hard French rolls and the sweet butter a perfect foil for them. Then cheese and "biscuits" (hard, unsalted, crackers), and the Camembert was smooth and creamy and the Dutch Blue sharp and mealy. We had to pass on dessert for none of us had any room left but the sweets cart had what looked like fruit tarts, cheese cake, trifle, and plum pudding as well as plates of rich and ornate butter cookies and fondant grapes. The demitasse was hot and strong and black enough to give you cause to repent and it was with a strong desire to stay on that we forced ourselves to leave in time to make a three o'clock date in London.

Unfortunately, the picture in the brochure does no justice to the interior of the Bel and the Dragon. There are six or seven small rooms besides the large dining room with French doors opening onto a small but exquisite garden. The doorways are low and narrow and the floor uneven but carpeted. Each room had a small coal grate purring away with a rosy glow. The tables were small and draped with snowy linen. In the private saloon, and keeping-room bars the tables all had pots of blooming hyacinths or crocus, and in the dining room each had a small bowl of red and purple anemones. Side tables here and there had enormous brass planters filled with greens or pine or flowers. They had hung their Christmas streamers of crepe paper and festooned the central fireplace with a string of colored lights. They waited on you hand and foot and I still can't figure out the protocol of service here. First the host greets you and turns you over to the head waiter who seats you. Then another tail-coated gent comes to take your bar order. Then another waiter comes to just look things over (guess he gives the all clear for the succeeding parade) and then the-waiter-who-takes-the-order appears and you inform him of your wishes with about forty-seven "Thank yous" thrown in. Then another waiter brings the proper service of silver and a while later still another brings hot plates. Finally a different one serves the food. Then the one who brought the silver clears off the finished course. Then the first waiter comes for another look and the whole routine is repeated with the addition of the wine-keeper who comes to take your order for fine wines and spirits. He doesn't pour your drinks, only supervises while a still different man opens and serves the bottles. This, together with the prodigious usage of serving dishes, would drive you bats. Everything has at least two service plates under it. The demitasse cup, for example, sits on its own small saucer on a four-inch plate on a ten-inch plate. Whoops, my dears, and them with no automatic dishwashers. No wonder there are so many scullery maids in England!

Now I must hoof it down to American Express. I could hop a bus or take a taxi but with the Christmas shoppers jamming the streets, it's easier to put on "me walkers" and use "me trotters"!

I'm getting fairly well familiar with London W.,1. and can find Bayswater Road, Oxford Street, Bond Street, Regents Street, Piccadilly Circus, Haymarket Street, Charing Cross Road, and Park Lane. These form a rough square about four miles in diameter and so far comprise my working world over here. Still haven't whipped the money situation, but am getting to where "seven and six" means something and can do a rough computation on how much, American, things cost. Bit of a nuisance, you know, but they haven't yorked me yet!

As far as our picture here, things came to a loud and violent crisis last week with the firing of our American writer and the employment of an English one. Elmo and I both got cranked up over that and being nailed to this flat for the past two weeks working together hasn't been good for our morale. In fact, I must confess, Sunday and yesterday Elmo and I were walking around here like two strange, stiff-legged, brindle bulldogs! Low growls and just waiting for the other guy to bite first. Need I tell you again how much good that raft of happy mail did us. Kerle commented about "poor timing"—if you only knew how perfect it was. By the time we had read each letter, laughed all the laughs, traded page for page, and talked over all your doings we were once more in accord. After three bleak grey days the sun shone inside and outside number 26 Hyde Park Gardens.

This morning we traded our homemade valentines and though our noses were a bit frosty, our hearts were warm again. Now I simply must beg off and get back to work on the script. Poor 'Mo—I got mad the last few days and staged an emotional strike. Being the stubborn Williams that he is, he undertook to write the script himself rather than apologize for some high-handed remarks. He has twisted and squirmed and sighed and ripped pages out of the typewriter and I feel like a dog for letting him go through such anguish. But maybe next time I hand him a rewrite he won't just grunt and say, "That's not right either!" I thought that if he knew the mental contortions involved, he would be a mite more sympathetic. Besides, when I get something so Elmo says it is ninety percent right, Tony comes by, reads it, and says it won't do at all for an English audience. When he blithely threw out my tender little love scene yesterday I could have wrapped the tea tray around his chubby little head! And the trouble is I can't argue back or say "boo" to defend it. This is undoubtedly the screwiest (if you'll pardon an old American word) set-up yet!

Enough of the complaining...it's part of what we go through on every picture. Lots of grief, lots of hard work, but soon forgotten once the film is in the can. Just don't let *anyone* kid you, though, that making movies is a glamorous and joy-filled profession.

We'll naturally be listening for the mail to plop through the mail slot so do keep writing. If I were home I'd give you all such a bear hug, I'd make Kerle's squeezes look sick! I love everybody dearly except I'm mad at Beau—two months and not even a post-card. If you don't write soon, my boy, I'm gonna start snortin and pawin and backin up for a run at you!

It must be time for tea; me stomach's growling. Whether or no, I'll have me a "cuppa" and drink a toast to the bestest family what is!

Happy Valentine to all of mine!

Love,
Lorraine

March, 1955

Dear Family,

With Elmo almost ready to reel off a mile and a half of dictation to me, I guess I will have to make this a carbon copy round-robin letter—not that there is much to write, but since mail coming our way has been falling off, I figure maybe I have been remiss about writing too. You'd be amazed at how sensitive our ears are for the lifting of the mail slot in the door. A beautiful sound!

Tomorrow being St. Patrick's day, I just tried to buy a bunch of real Irish shamrocks to send to Pop but found out, to my chagrin, I'd be forbidden to mail them. And they were such cute little rascals too. In fact, I had a bad morning of it shopping. Had a real routine buying a new typewriter ribbon (but forgot to get any new carbon paper—sorry!) and ended up thinking the British just expect things to naturally be the wrong size, shape, color and be unable to get them for a fortnight even so. Brother, what a good dose of American efficiency would do over here! It would be such a rude shock, though, that the whole damned island would probably sink. At any suggestion to improve their merchandising, their income, or their methods, they shrug politely and say, "Oh, well, you *Ameddicuns* are *teddibly* ambitious, don't you know, but we have managed for quite a long time!" I honestly think they are very proud of inefficiency and discomfort as though placidly enduring inconveniences is proof of their strength and virility.

I wanted very much to observe an excellent little French pastry shop near here so I could teach Axel and Mom what I might learn—just some new wrinkles on fancy pastries and decorations. Oh no! Even if I paid for the privilege, it "just wasn't done," "frightfully inconvenient," "cooks are temperamental," and so on and on. I wanted to make some of those plastic ball and toothpick gimmicks to give to friends here for centerpieces (they'd think they were hotsy-totsy for sure), but the florist never heard of plastic foam and they just gave me the big blank look all through my descriptions. This morning they have violets, daffodils, and tulips for sale; you either buy violets, daffodils, or tulips, or to hell with you! Came home loaded down with groceries to find the lift wasn't working and had to hoof it up five flights. Neighbor says it is a common occurrence, was out of operation six weeks last year and for no specific reason except the yearly license expired and it took the examiner that long to come around. Meanwhile the porter pulled the master control switch so no one would use it in the interim. Must have everything proper, don't you know?

Sounds like I'm mad at England; no, I'm really not. They have a number of things far better than ours. Today I just happened to have a run of not-too-good things. For instance, people who are learning to drive a car, a motorcycle, or even ride a bicycle must fasten a plaque with a large "L" on the front and back of their vehicle and keep it there for six months. Great idea: you see a car with an "L" sign on it and give the driver a little more consideration and a wider berth than normal. Dogs can ride on busses which is sensible so long as they sit quietly on their owners' lap. Fine for the Peke and poodle crowd, but quite a surprise to sit down next to an enormous boxer and worry if there really is someone underneath him.

As I think I told you before, cars only drive with parking lights at night within the city, brights are only turned on for a second if you turn into a particularly dark side street. It is amazing, too, how much you can see, but I still wonder that more black-coated pedestrians aren't run down. The taxis, busses, and underground trains situations are amazingly efficient and very reasonable. People are very good-natured about the rush-hour jams and I've had some of my best conversations while waiting in a bus queue. Oftentimes a beggar musician (of which there are many) will come up alongside and play show tunes on his accordion or fiddle. Once in awhile the people will start to sing, and everyone drops a penny or two in his cap just before the bus finally pulls up. No smoking on the lower deck of the bus, but smoking on the upper so everyone is pleased. And the conductors and conductresses are very friendly when you ask directions. In fact, half the people generally get into the discussion as to which corner you should get off and which turning you should take, and you end up with so much direction you are completely confused.

Now Elmo is ready for me to go to work for him. We start shooting in eight days and there is, as always, eighty days' work to do. He is at the "deep sighs and pacing the floor" stage but grimly determined to stick it out. So me and the bicarb will do all we can to help. Please write when you can—a letter from home is like a bright sunny day over here—rare and wonderful!

Love,
Lorraine

March 21st (I theenk!), 1955

Dear Family,

That's a heck of a note for sure. I honestly don't know what date it is—or which week for that matter. I lined the garbage can with the London Times this morning and I certainly am not going to dig through all the tea leaves and left-over brussel sprouts to try and find out. The way things have been going lately it won't make a whit of difference. We have both really had our noses to the grindstone, and—wouldn't you know it—the weather has been knocking itself out. Oh, it's still cold—"fresh"—as our friends here call it, but the sun has been shining merrily every day and it seems mighty good to see a blue and white clouded sky instead of the London grey akin to the charcoal hue! Our share in this glorious spring weather has been to watch the pigeons preening and strutting on our window ledge after their breakfast and to sit at breakfast and enjoy the sunshine on our backs as it comes through the window. Outside of that, we have worked, worked, worked. And this is only the beginning of the intensity part of it all. Elmo and I are half way through a production break-down which means drawing diagrams and writing descriptions of every shot and every scene. In other words, "directing" the whole film on paper first. It is one whale of a job but one that certainly contributes to a great deal of peace of mind and never has any job been over-prepared.

They are having great trouble casting. Lippert tried to get Ida Lupino, then Marilyn Maxwell, and then Evelyn Keyes after our hopes of getting Jan Sterling faded. No soap on these three lovelies either and Tony and Elmo and the gentlemen Carreras are all very disappointed. Under stimulus of Elmo's enthusiasm they were all digging in and even preparing to spend some additional money provided the name value of a fairly good actress could be added. With this news today, I doubt if they even put toilet paper in the W.C. at the studio now!

Elmo has had his "bug" something fierce and I keep spooning yoghurt and soft diet into him, then we go out for an evening and he can't bear to hurt anyone's feelings and eats a lot of indigestibles and starts the routine all over again. Over the weekend I practically put my foot on the back of his neck trying to get him healthy and primed to start shooting this coming Wednesday. Now tonight he has gone into the office to meet some of the actors and actresses. I'll bet anything they either go to a pub or to a restaurant, and if he comes home with a bellyache, I'm gonna BLIP him a good one. Still I can't help but believe this condition, recurring as it always does in times of stress and worry, has a great deal to do with his mental outlook. He claims it is a wrong combination of foods; I claim it is chemical imbalance induced by fretting too much and too long. Whatever it is, I wish it would go the hell away!

While Elmo has been on a restricted diet, I put me on one too, not because I wasn't feeling well but I was busting out all over. Holy smoke, what this five-a-day routine can do to you. Have got my belts back in their normal notch by now but want to hang on another day or two if I can.

We start shooting Wednesday and will whack away at it until the 29th of April. Since the next day will be Elmo's birthday and a Saturday, I'm going to try and arrange an end-of-picture party in his honor.

This Saturday we have tickets to the Grand National Steeple Chase at Aintree which is up near Liverpool in the northernmost part of the island. It is the *big race* of the European continent—of the world as a matter of fact. I'm so excited I don't dare think about it. It is costing us a fortune to go since we had to buy honorary memberships to the clubhouse in order to get seats and round-trip tickets on the special train were twelve pounds ($36.00) alone but including four meals. If I can pick the winner and get a quid on his nose, we may come out even, but if not it will still be a wonderful and rare experience.

I wish I had more news to write about this week but, gosh darn it, we have hardly poked our noses out of the door. In fact, we have hardly got up from table and typewriter. This is the time in the picture business when you wish you ran a gas station—so much to do—so many factors altering script and story—so many people working without any apparent coordination, and you so blamed tired of the whole shebang you wonder how you are ever going to hang on through production let alone be sparkling, scintillating, and inspire good performances from cast and crew! If Elmo were a drinking man I'd take him out on a good bender—we both could use one—but instead I'll compromise by trying to get him to bed early and making him watch his diet and hope for the best.

I must confess that I am now getting excited over the picture—my spirits go UP when Elmo's go DOWN. Don't know why except he tends to be overly pessimistic and I figure, anyway, this is just a dumb "B" picture, so what the...!

A person can try and try and try and give more than his all and factors can be against you. If you just learn to live and let go and do what you can when you can—like a friend said, "It will come from left field." Well, here goes me trotting out into position.

Love you all—must get back to work!

Lorraine

April 3, 1955

Dear Family,

It's a confused sort of morning over here. The sun is flirting with some puffy grey clouds so it can either be dampish or dry. Hasn't bothered the pigeons, though, since they have cleaned us out of two pie tins full of bread scraps already and it isn't quite nine o'clock. Even so, I had to save out a cupful for my pet "door knocker" who must have some William's heritage 'cause he doesn't make it around before teatime. I keep telling him "the early bird" (and all that sort of rot), but he just cocks his head and gives me the sad orange eye and off I trot to crumble up some of Elmo's precious soda crackers or share my teatime toast with him.

Elmo is working on script breakdown at the dining room table and I am trying to whack out a mess of letters before it is time for me to type up three copies of same. So if this letter is interrupted, please understand. The boss has work for me.

Last week was one of mixed emotions as you can guess. By Wednesday I had worked myself up to the hives-and-hiccups state of nervous anticipation. Elmo was so engrossed and exhausted by the long hard hours he had been putting in that he, fortunately, just didn't have time or energy to get excited about the Academy Awards. We figured the actual ceremony would be taking place at about four in the morning Thursday, London time. So I primed myself to wake up and give a big think about all of you gathered there and wishing, with me, for him. Waited for the sound wave of an exultant shout to reach me by mental telepathy but it didn't come, and I somehow figured he hadn't won a companion for the gold boy on the coffee table. I stayed home Thursday just in case a cable should come and promised to phone Elmo immediately.

By noon I had worn holes in the carpet, smoked up a storm, run out of coffee, eaten all the toffees, and couldn't stand it a minute longer. We are also in the middle of a newspaper strike here so no papers this past week. In a rush of inspiration I phoned Associated Press and told them my story. And that's how I found out that Gene Milford had won for *On The Waterfront*. As much as I felt letdown I was still happy for Gene since it was his first Oscar and I shall never forget the thrill that comes with that. Now we shall all have to be happy for him and firmly believe that Elmo will someday garner another. I debated and debated about phoning, but knowing Elmo was having his toughest day's shooting I held off. He came home looking like a whipped pup—frozen, white-faced, discouraged, and dead tired. I dreaded giving him the bad news but he had already heard through *Exclusive*. That wasn't the cause for his weariness, though, but the murderous day he had spent working outside in a forty-mile gale with cast, crew, and fifty extras and four crying babies. He said it was like the worst of the *Tall Texan* days but bitterly cold. About the best I could do was poke the electric heater in the bathroom, run him a scalding hot bath, wrap him up in sweaters, robes, overcoat, and wool sox, and bury him under a mound of comforters and quilts and feed him some milk toast. By the time I took the bowl away he just rolled over and gave up. A good night's sleep and he was ready to go again. Fortunately, they don't work Saturdays here so Friday night I beat his ears to make him go to bed at seven-thirty—you know how stubborn he is. So I said we'd both go to bed and read. Foxy me—about fifteen minutes later his eyes were shut and he was snoring gently into the pages of *Readers Digest*. I took the magazine away, turned out the lights, and came back in the living room. He didn't stir until ten o'clock Saturday morning and when he started whistling "The Meadowlark Song" while he shaved I knew things were looking up again.

And since yesterday was a "golden" morning and spring was practically pushing up the paving stones, we stole half a day off to go shopping. I had been to Liberty's Department Store on Friday and, believe me, I could write a glowing five-page letter on this gem alone. World famous for fabrics, you can actually get sick from the emotional impact of such unbelievably gorgeous things. As Willie knows, they have an excellent picture department and the girls had promised me when they were here that if I'd come back after inventory they would show me all the prints and watercolors they had for sale. Well, I discovered the watercolors of a man named Weisbrod, a Swiss, and just about flipped. Such power and vitality and yet an ability to create almost any mood in a painting. They had about 20 of his things, unframed, and only moderately expensive for good originals. Well, I couldn't choose since I liked them all and decided that Elmo simply must see them.

So Saturday about ten we headed for Liberty's. I made the mistake of taking him in through the door in the Men's Shop so we paused and within half an hour had spent all our mad money for a handsome charcoal and pink waistcoat and five simply smashing ties. Going toward the stairway Elmo spotted some gossamer-soft handwoven stoles and was determined to buy one, then and there, for Mom. Counted our pounds and pennies in the corner, and Mom will have to wait a bit—next paycheck for sure. Then up to the picture department and I just dug out and opened the Weisbrod portfolio and stood back. If ever you saw a man go into a trance, that was Elmo. I left and walked a few blocks to the tobacconist for some smokes, detoured to the ladies' room, went downstairs and walked though the lamp department, sat in a corner and smoked, walked over to the greeting cards and chose some to frame...and he *never once* missed me.

Coming home, walking through the park, he said "You know, if we can figure out how to do it, we probably ought to buy that street scene—if only for an investment!" No kidding, we both were so impressed with this man's work that we believe he might become famous one day soon. Strangely enough he is an extremely wealthy and successful business man; he owns the Zussa Silk mills in Switzerland and has many textile holdings in British companies. According to the girl who heads the department there, he is utterly charming and as vital and exciting a person as his paintings would indicate.

By the time we got back to the flat it was time to cook up some supper, tie into some work on the script breakdown and pile into the sack at an early hour again. As a consequence we are both up bright and early this morning and feeling so good that I didn't even grumble at having to unscramble Lady's Cunninghame's poor excuse of a bed and go through the tortuous ritual of putting sheets, eight blankets (thin ones) and two comforters, three pillows, and two tatty brocade spreads in their proper overlapped positions.

Ta! Ta! for now.
Lorraine

April, 1955

London *heah*!

Having frittered away the entire day in most delightful aimless wanderings, I shall proceed to spend this last hour before Elmo gets home for supper letting some words wander onto paper for a visit with you. Oh, there were all sorts of chores I should have been doing today, but with bright sunshine beckoning and spring bursting out all over, who could resist? Not I at any rate.

Spring does literally burst out in England. One day all the trees and shrubs are black and grimy growths just twisting up out of the bare earth. Then, a few days sunshine and warmth and *suddenly* the trees are pale green smudges against the sky, those stubby hedges are dazzling gold forsythia, and that straggly little tree by the corner is throwing pink almond blossoms all over the sky. Then the poodles and pugs and plain dogs that take their "mornings" and "evenings" in the park go leaping and barking off like they have suddenly gone insane. And the cats come out from spending the winter in front of the coal fire and sun themselves on the doorsills and porch posts. Mommies put the babies out in their prams to enjoy the nice air and hundreds of nannies take their small charges to the park to frolic. Fusty, musty old gentlemen lovingly carry their miniature sailboats to the ponds in Hyde Park and put them down at one end, trim the sails, and let them go while they and their gentlemen cronies walk at a leisurely pace around the pond to pick the boats up at the other end and sail them back again.

This past weekend was one of England's three legal bank-day holidays. Everything stopped while the north of England went south, the south went west, the west went east, and Elmo and I got caught in the middle of the traffic jam. With Tony Hinds, our young producer, we drove to Wales. Funny thing, I thought we were going south to Kent or Sussex but only found out after I was "tucked" (I learned that's the right word) that Tony couldn't get reservations in the south so we were going north. Weather reports had been for cold and rainy weather and there was I with only a light coat since with all the fellow's camera gear, space was really at a premium. Turned out alright since I wore Elmo's longhandle tops under my dress and wrapped a wool scarf around my legs when we were driving. The car had no heater and a terrible draft so we all three were more than willing to stop very often for a cuppa tea or a pinta beer. Even so, all in all, we had our share of sunny weather and a completely hilarious good time.

We left early Friday morning and returned late Monday night. I whomped up breakfast for 5a.m. and we were on the road by a quarter to six. With many stops for you-know-what, meals, and picture-taking, we reached our first night's destination at Tyn-y-coed by six that night. A good lukewarm bath, dressed for dinner, and a supper that warmed the cockles of your heart and the three of us headed straight for bed.

Like good kids we were up bright and early next morning only to find that breakfast would not be served "under any circumstances" until nine o'clock. So we went walking, rummaged in the back of the car and settled our ravenous tummies somewhat with cookies and oranges, and just barely managed until we heard the breakfast gong, whereupon we stormed the dining room to the utter merriment of the waitresses. We checked out of the hotel, visited a lovely waterfall called Swallow Falls, and headed for the curving, twisting byways of Wales. The names of the towns are charming but absolutely guaranteed unpronounceable to the Yankee tongue. Just in case you think I was kidding with Tyn-y-coed earlier, then try wrapping your tonsils around Llangollen, pronounced exactly the way a cat sounds when it sneezes. If you want to try it, imagine that a crumb had stuck at the back of your throat and you are about to strangle and give a quick little cough to get rid of it. Ready? That makes Llangollen sound like "kclan—kochlen" which isn't easy no matter how you say it.

When I was a little girl and heard of the Prince of Wales, I thought they were talking about whales. Now that I was grown-up I knew I wouldn't see any whales, but still labored under the mistaken idea that all Welchmen sang all the time. Knowing that the leek, that great big overgrown onion, was their natural insignia, I was sure I'd be served leek soup by singing waiters but, there again, I was disillusioned. Each meal was a replica of regular English cooking and I never heard so much as a peep of singing. Tony says they are so poor in Wales there is nothing much to sing about. Being primarily a farming and sheep raising country in the north and a mining country in the south, Wales is not so prosperous as the rest of the British Isles. But what it lacks in money it makes up for in beauty. This is the mountainous section of the country and most picturesque. Of course Mount Snowdon, the pride of every Welshman, is only just over three thousand feet but, to them, that is tremendous indeed. The whole countryside is laid out in fields bounded with shale stone fences and walls. It is the greenest green you could ever imagine.

We stopped just outside Capel Curig to photograph a sheepherder and his wife and dogs moving a band of sheep and they told us they had had over 140 inches of rain that year already! That's why you want to wear waterproof shoes when you go walking—the whole turf is spongy and springs and rivulets go rushing off in every direction.

One's impressions of Wales are these I would say: brilliant extravagant green, picturesque stone cottages and huddled together villages, narrow winding roads that twist over hills and wiggle down valleys with vistas in every direction of stone-bordered fields full of ewes and lambs, clusters of daffodils thriving in half the nooks and corners and sort of an all-pervading feeling that you must be dreaming such a storybook countryside.

I *never* saw so many sheep in my life. Each and every one of those fields had its share of ewes and lambs. And such adorable lambs—newborns standing spraddle-legged and wide-eyed by their mothers, lambs sleeping, lambs nursing and, cutest of all, lambs gamboling. When they get a couple of weeks old they get frisky and chum up with some of their contemporaries for the wildest lamb games you ever did see—such leaping into the air and baaa-ing and chasing one another and mock butting contests. We often just stopped the car and sat watching them frolic. In fact, looking back on our visit to Wales, about all I can see in my mind's eye are sheep and sheep and lambs and lambs. Which brings me to the point that it is now time to say GOOD BAAAAAAA!

Love,
Lorraine

April, 1955

Dear Family,

Saturday night and have we been howling! Elmo quit cutting at nine o'clock since his eyes were almost burned out after two weeks' steady 16-hour days. I was here in the room pounding out letters and trying to catch up on a month's neglect when home he came. So we just up and did us a "do". Went for a walk, got completely turned around, which is inevitable in London and ended up back at Victoria station around the corner. Bought two magazines, two packets of cigarettes (Piccadilly's for me, Players for him), stopped in for a cuppa tea and here we are at ten-thirty, beat and bushed and heading for bed. I was going to write you anyway, but now Elmo has added impetus to impulse since he said there were some questions in your last letter that needed answering.

Here goes:

First off, Disney's version of an Oscar featuring Mickey Mouse is called a "Mouscar". Hang on to it. It has cost us a lot of grief already. Seems that when Elmo didn't get the Oscar, Walt Disney was so disappointed that he decided that Elmo should have some sort of reward after all for the superlative job (Walt's words) that he did. Mouscar is it and Walt was kind enough to send it to us in England. Ah ha! But before we could get it there were several little matters: import-export license, customs declarations, intent of purposes, statement of value, appraisal estimates, etc., etc., etc. Three days later and forty-five forms signed and mailed to the airport I get the second letter. Now all they want is twenty pounds (sixty bucks) duty plus a few minor storage and impoundment and inspection fees. I blew. Elmo blew. I phoned BOAC and found out how much to ship Mouscar home, sight, by us, unseen. Four pounds—okay—so give the little rascal a pat on the head for us, and tell him he ain't always gonna be an orphink!

Secondly, that goldanged bill from Motion Picture Herald for $140.00 makes us both so mad we could spit in the editor's eye from over here. Hold it and Elmo will shrivel a telephone line when he gets back. No matter how often you tell these birds not to they will run those things and then bill you in hopes you will be shamed into paying. Nuts! I'm getting tired of that kind of publicity since I doubt if it does any good, and besides we certainly don't like being pressured!

Finally, current events. Elmo is just now winding up his first cut on the prison film. The ravings have subsided to mutters and, if he can only figure out how to wangle a flash-back within a flash-back, he may be able to salvage the love scene and cutaway to the boy. It ain't easy but if anyone can do it, Elmo can. He screens the picture Monday and I will see it for the first time then. Not because I am such a privileged person but because they need some more dialogue written. UGH!

Script-wise I am betwixt and between. Got my five copies back from the typing service and Elmo handed them out around the office. Tonight Elmo returned with Tony's copy and his written critique; his opinion is that I'm short on story but solid on dialogue and characterization. I knew the former all along but, inspired by his compliments and Elmo's sort of dazzled recognition of them, I am most encouraged to buckle down Monday to improving storyline. Will you permit me to quote from Tony's note? After all it is the first compliment I have had in six months. Well, here it is, boy, oh boy, oh boy!

"I have not been hypnotized by the almost overpowering strength of writing of the descriptive passages in this script when I say that the quality of the writing has elevated what was definitely a pretty "B" script to a very much top ranking "A". Most important to my taste, Lorraine, is that the characters are now all honest and not merely ciphers dragged from the stock drawer."

Lawks, kids, that oughtta hold me for the next six months!

On that happy, happy note I shall drift quite blissfully off the subject. Later on I'll get back to my normal cussing self.

(Later on...)

Kids, the clock on Her Majesty's stables just tink-tonked eleven. This kid is tired so I shall sign off. Elmo just strolled in from taking a hot bath wearing raincoat and hat over nylon pajamas and bare feet. Don't ask *me* why—I think he has slipped another cog.

We are getting anxious to get home. Won't admit it but we are. Tomorrow we shall steal a couple of hours of sunshine and maybe catch an excursion boat for a ride up the Thames and back. Then Elmo to the cutting room and me to the typewriter. And still planning to sail on the 16th. Hot diggity dog.

Love,
Lorraine

May, 1955

Dear Family,

Another in the Round-Robin series and with so much to write about we don't quite know where to start. After Elmo finished up the picture, it seemed a good idea to get as far away from all the work and worries of the past few months as possible. So we 'opped the plane to Stavanger, Norway in company with Tony Hinds, our young producer. A beautiful three-hour flight and down at the spacious airport of this little Norwegian fishing town and a bus ride into the Atlantic Hotel in the city. Don't know if the Atlantic Hotel was such a good idea or not; it was a magnificent introduction to a holiday, the most modern, the most gracious. And with the finest cuisine of any hotel we have ever visited. It was a great welcome, especially since our arrival coincided with Liberation Day (when the English and Americans arrived ten years before after driving out the Germans who had cruelly occupied Norway since shortly after W.W. II began), and the staff and guests were determined to knock themselves out retelling how glad they were to see us then and now. Every window in the town had a candle burning in it to signify the bonfires built to guide the planes and ships in safely. It was most touching and several hours' conversation with the manager and some of the guests made us all realize what an ordeal the peoples of occupied countries had lived through.

Sunday we roamed through the town taking pictures in spite of persistent drizzles but returning every half whipstitch for another round of eating. Such food. The Atlantic is most unusual in that it was built by private conscription and does not operate at a profit. Seems the two dozen or so tremendously wealthy fish cannery operators wanted a nice place to live and entertain when in town so they ante'ed up the price and each man keeps a suite reserved for himself. Not without reason, though, the hotel has become the social center of the entire community with a gorgeous dance-and-dining room, a separate ballroom, four small reception rooms, an enormous lobby, and a downstairs restaurant with an outside garden room overlooking the street and the lake. When we picked up the bill after the two nights Elmo was all for throwing the idea of continuing on to the winds and just staying PUT! He was in his private gourmet's heaven what with exquisite poached cold salmon, sliced hothouse cucumber, and *loads* of hollandaise sauce, flaky white rolls, sweet country butter, and a tray of pastries that would make Mom throw up her hands in pure delight! (Lorraine almost drowned in coffee but managed to soak most of it up with Danish pastries before the worst happened.)

Sunday night we took the little steamer that threads its way through the fjords up to Bergen. And after the enormous supper we packed away at the hotel, we still peeked into the dining saloon on the boat. There was spread a lavish smorgasbord. Well, Tony likes to eat too, and there was one horrible moment when the three of us got wedged into the doorway trying to get in first. Since Lorraine was the lady (and that might be questioned) in the party, Elmo and Tony fell to fighting politely at the rear leaving her to lead the way around. When we made "wanting to pay" signs the waitress shook her head emphatically and indicated this spread was on Norway, the steward shook hands all around, the other patrons beamed indulgently on the three squirrel-cheeked visitors who then lurched groaningly to bed. Slept like three logs. There is something about a bellyful of fishloaf, meatballs, cheese, and pickles that does it.

Up at the crack of dawn next day to roam the boat and watch the unloading and loading procedures at the many small villages we stopped at and after breakfast (natch!) which was a repeat of the smorgasbord with boiled eggs and bacon added, we lurched off to Bergen for the day. Deposited bags at the railway depot and went off to take pictures and find a coffee shop. At four that afternoon we caught the bus for Norheimsund and had a panoramic ride through some breathtaking mountain country. Wonderful bus, wonderful people, including an ancient countryman who had had a few too many beers in town and had to be scolded by the bus driver for singing too loudly to himself in the back seat. After the talking-to, I thought the old man was going to cry, but at a coffee stop a little later the driver bought him a coffee and a plate of hash and cordial relationships were once again effected. We reached Norheimsund at seven-thirty and were delighted to find our hotel was sitting right at the edge of the fjord.

No need to describe Norheimsund, the hotel, the houses, the waterfall, the country lanes, or the rowboats, or the lambs and ewes—we have about six rolls of 35mm stills taken from every conceivable angle and under similar weather conditions in the five days we were there. Suffice it to say any descriptions we might tender would be inadequate anyway since the place is a combination of Disney cartoon idealization and the kind of charming countryside we all would like to retire to someday. People were delightful to us, the hotel staff so gracious and smiling, the other guests affable, and even the local residents who couldn't speak English (most Norwegians do, though) smiled and waved and pantomimed and shrugged and had a cigarette with us. We learned to say phonetically, *"viss-i-oed"* and *"tak"* which are "please" and "thank you" and both words got a thorough workout every day. Our fellow guests were a honeymoon couple from Manchester, England, a group of four little plain-Jane shopgirls from Liverpool, a Norwegian traveling salesman (delighted to practice his English on us), and a retired Yank army officer and his pleasant Puerto Rican wife. The last night happened to be the birthday of one of the Liverpudlian girls and since, no doubt, they had dreamt dreams of meeting handsome eligible men on their long saved-for holiday, the management (bless their hearts) arranged a party in their honor, invited in some of the local teenagers, got Nordic Viking youths for dates for the girls, and us "old folks" sat around the lobby applauding and sipping beer while youth had its waltzes and a few rounds of folk dances.

Leaving Norheimsund in the proper travelogue fashion, we had a glorious sunset ride by coastal steam to Ulvig for the next night's stop. Here a magnificent new half-glass hotel has been built on the ruins of the old 1840 establishment burnt by the retreating Germans. It was almost too much for us after the rustic family feeling we had known at Norheimsund. Too push-button, too much cocktail party atmosphere, too theatrical to somehow fit in this idyllic setting...the town almost plunked in the lap of a valley with the fjord waters lapping at its toes, majestic mountains rising all around gently behind the town, but alarmingly straight up out of the neck of the fjord. Early next morning the lake was a silver sheet of quicksilver, the mists were floating up the hills to gradually reveal blue sky and whipped cream clouds. Everything was washed fresh by rain and crisp as a garden cucumber. The birds were rehearsing for spring around the corner, the kids were pedaling furiously uphill and down on their way to school, mamas were washing windows already and shoving armfuls of down comforters over the upper windowsills to air, and papas were hiking down to town for a package of tobacco and a bucket of milk. Tony was out for a row on the lake and his little boat looked like a leaf on a table mirror. Elmo was going f.2 and a third of a second crazy to get the right exposure for a shot he wanted, and Lorraine was puffing up and down hills trying to keep up with him. Let's hope the pictures gratify his artistic nature and justify the five miles of mountain climbing that we accomplished in the hour before our bus got in.

Then to Oslo, the capitol, and into the Hotel Viking (pronounced "Vicking") for the big national holiday celebration, Constitution Day, to commemorate the separation of Sweden and Norway in 1905. The weather threatened rain but held fair so the outdoor *beergarden* restaurants were filled and the ships in the harbor were decorated with flapping flags and pennants. All the little kids (and Lorraine) carried a Norwegian flag. Elmo and Tony sported red, white, and blue lapel rosettes. Everyone smiled and nodded at us and we smiled and nodded right back.

Went out to photograph the big parade next day. All the school children of Oslo congregate at their various schools in the city and begin parading towards the King's Palace until finally they all meet in one tremendous procession going up the esplanade together, singing and waving their flags and circling through the palace drives. The Royal Family stands waving back on their balcony and, after the official parade is over, the impromptu ones begin. These are mainly organized by the students of high school and university age and seem to center around the ancient automobiles they buy, invariably painted firetruck red, and emblazoned with all sorts of signs, fringed canvas covers, and loaded with shrieking, horn-blowing, yelling hordes of good-looking boys and girls. I'm afraid the camera record of the celebration will consist of a long shot of the palace with a blooming tree in the foreground and innumerable close shots of little kids. I have *never* seen such handsome kids and all togged out in new outfits and bright spirits. Uncle Elmo was in his glory and even Tony, a determined bachelor, was overwhelmed to the extent of ignoring the pageantry in favor of the toddlers.

Since there were such mobs of people out and it is no easy task trying to keep two photographers together, we decided to rendezvous at one of the lovely outdoor restaurants in case we were separated. Good old Tony! We'd lose him about every two hours which was delightful for it meant another stop for either beer and those classic open-face sandwiches the Norwegians love or coffee and pastry and two pieces of whipped cream cake for Elmo. In every way, and especially gustatorially and photographically, our Norwegian visit was *a pip*!

Then to Sweden via another lovely S.A.S. flight and into the city that is rightly called the Venice of the North. Spent the next day in enchanted bewilderment at the City Hall of Stockholm. And the following two days window-shopping and visiting Skansen, the island park which is authentic 15th Century Sweden. Watched the polar bears in the Skansen zoo playing polar bear games with some old billiard balls that some genius had contributed to their swimming pool. Watched the elk eat the bark off the birch tree branches and fed the squirrels and the ducks at the ponds and rubbed the newborn calf that had been born to the black and white milk cow at one of the recreated farms. Hated to leave Stockholm just as we had hated to leave Oslo, but that's the way a good vacation goes.

Had our last Saturday night and Sunday in Copenhagen. Dined at the world famous Tivoli Gardens, listened to the open-air dance bands and the symphony orchestra and walked home with only the lights of the harbor for our company. Sunday we took pictures like crazy again and window-shopped along the main streets, hurried to the airport for our London flight, and once more flew up above the clouds into the sun that keeps shining at these northern countries until eleven-thirty at night.

Came home to London in such full spring glory that for a while we wondered if we hadn't been fools to leave it. The chestnut trees are like giant candelabra holding up their white blossoms, the tulips and rhododendrons are in full glory, the baby ducks have hatched in St. James Park and I have to walk over every afternoon and watch them learn to dive. They get *so* mad because they can't get their little cork bottoms under no matter how hard they kick. Elmo almost falls off the bridge laughing so our daily walk in the park has now become a necessity.

We both have plenty of problems connected with work—the picture, according to Elmo, is lousy and he is hammering away in the cutting room. The script for the Mexican film is ditto so Lorraine is hammering away at the typewriter. Even so, in spite of the discouragement we feel on these two projects we can't get too low in spirits seeing what fun we have had and are having.

We came to the conclusion in summing up our vacation that Norway has the scenery, Sweden the city (Stockholm), but the Danes have the system! Will elaborate to all who are interested when we get home.

Love from,
Elmo and Lorraine

May, 1955

Dear One and All,

When our stay in London was winding down, Elmo surmised correctly that the days of the great ocean liners were also winding down and that before air travel took over completely, I should have the luxury of a first class crossing on the fabled Queen Mary. Accordingly, we gave up our flat, packed up all the many take-homes my visits to Portobello Road and Bermondsey Market had gleaned, and entrained for Southhampton. In spite of our most proper attire as we boarded that stately behemoth vessel, we did garner a smile or two since space had necessitated our each carrying one long brass coach horn over each shoulder. But in deference to their pacifying affect in times of turmoil, we considered them not only attractive, but vital. Besides, in our cabin, they made lovely side panels to the huge, handled basket of spring flowers our loving friend, Anna Neagle, Britain's top star, had sent me. We unpacked, hung up our clothes, changed for dinner and strolled the decks until the chimes for first seating rang. The stewards in the dining room were apologetic, "Negotiations, don't you know," so a rather meager cold collation was laid out. Still it sufficed, especially with a bottle of bubbly and the Fortnum and Mason chocolates also gifted by friends. And so, contented, to bed. We woke in the early morning to a shudder of engines. A quick dress and race topside to watch the gangplank being lifted. A long wait and the gangplank was replaced and the engines sighed to a stop. Then that dreaded word "strike" echoed out of the loudhailers and, at that moment, some eight hundred of us were shipless, and unless accommodations could be found back in London, homeless as well. Everyone packed up, loaded up, boarded buses, all on a few meager sandwiches and pot of tea. Fortunately, the sandwiches weren't sardine (but the passengers were, especially one dimwit couple, literally hidden behind suitcases). And in our case, add the coach horns and that enormous bouquet that I refused to leave behind.

This time, arriving in London, I was not crisp and groomed wearing an orchid corsage. I was, instead, almost as drooping as the bouquet I carried. Elmo galloped off, coach horns over shoulder, to try and find transport and some place to be transported to. And it was the indomitable cockney humor that saved us, "Oi, mate," a cabby shouted, wheeling around to Elmo heading for the perpetual queue, "lost the rest of yer band?" After he nodded us aboard came the question of where to find digs before the rest of the some six thousand shipless souls got there first. Knowing that all the first class hotels would be booked solid, we also knew that, having purchased the extravagance of the Queen, we had to settle for a much more modest bed down. So our friend headed for the back streets and pulled up in front of the Hotel Rubens, directly across from Buckingham Palace Mews. They were happy to have us but not nearly as happy as I would be, for had we not been turned back to London, I would never have met two gentlemen, Prince Phillip and my battling waiter, who left me with vivid and endearing impressions.

To afford even the modest expense of the Rubens meant work for one or both of us so Elmo moved back into the Soho cutting rooms of Hammer Films and plied the trade he plied so well. I went back to the traveling typewriter and a western script that to this day has never been finished. Ah well, I only mention it because one night I had written a scene about members of a wagon train crossing dangerous open country and barely escaping an encounter with marauding Indians. It was a good scene, so good that it scared the wits out of me. I came down with a mingled case of writer's fatigue and a certainty that Kiowas were about to come whooping out of the clothes closet. So I phoned Elmo and he said to catch a bus and come on down to the cutting room for, by the time I arrived, he could wrap up his work for the day and we'd get a bite to eat and walk back to the hotel. Now this innocent broad, having never been in the Soho sector of London at night, did not realize why those attractive young ladies were strolling about or standing in doorways. So, after ringing the night bell at the Hammer offices, knowing I'd have to wait a spell for Elmo to exit the cutting room on the fifth floor and make his way down, I leaned in the corner of the doorway. Within two minutes I was ringed by three irate, fire-spitting French-speaking women. I couldn't understand what they were planning on doing to me but I knew it wasn't going to be enjoyable. When Elmo finally opened the door and it was apparent I was only waiting for my man and not for ones they considered theirs, they backed off. I had that evening escaped from two savage packs and, in retrospect, the Kiowas were the lesser of the two.

As for my encounter with that distinguished gentleman, husband to the Queen and purveyor of goodwill throughout the land, it came about by the lovely accident of stopping for a late lunch one Sunday with good friends, Tony and Michael, at the Hinds Head in Bray. The other diners had departed and it was only the kindness of the proprietress, Mrs. Williams, who not only saw that we were fed but joined us at table. When Prince Phillip entered, he greeted our hostess with warmth and reached across the table to shake hands with Michael whom he also knew. Hungry himself, he joined us and within minutes had ascertained that Elmo was not only American but from the southwest, obviously horse country.

And so the stories began; polo ponies, quarter horses, mustangs, Tennessee walkers and thoroughbreds all had their trot by, culminating with great laughter at the predicaments Michael had known in his days as one of the Horse Guards. These handsome and aristocratic young men, accoutered in white buckskin breeches, hip-high glossy boots, scarlet jerkins and brass breastplates, sit statue-still on their polished mounts rump-backed into those little sentry boxes outside Whitehall. Part of their mystique is that they must never waiver, never glance right nor left, up nor down, no matter what. Michael confessed, however, how much they enjoyed the love notes that young ladies dropped into the tops of their boots and that it was no problem to remember which correspondent was the prettiest and thus deserving of a reply. The greatest bane, though, was the habit of dear elderly ladies who, feeling these brave young defenders of the Empire must be hungry, contributed chocolate bars to the boots and necessitated the purchase of yet another expensive pair of white buckskin breeches. Michael said they always had the long time of sitting motionless, feeling the chocolate melt and dribble down their shins, to reflect upon the deficit to egos as well as their purses.

Before the luncheon concluded, Prince Phillip remarked that he had been out to the aerodrome taking a flying lesson for, even though he was licensed for aircraft, he had lately taken to getting around by helicopter and wanted to be able to pilot it himself. Whereupon I remarked that I was well aware of his new mode of transport since his craft invariably took off from behind the Buckingham Palace Mews, lifted laboriously over the stables and did a very close fly-by to our hotel window. Then, gallant gentleman that he is, he promised to wave at me whenever passing. And, do you know what? He always did.

My battling waiter was a gentleman too, as well as another horse lover. Only instead of riding horses, he bet on them with a passion and intensity that saw him running out the back door of the Ruben's kitchen to his bookmaker whenever a sufficient tip should come his way. Since Elmo was now working most nights and I would dine alone, he opened the ante with a rather large donation to insure that I should have good service. And I also remember to tip just that tiny bit better than the usual run of out-of-town businessmen or country folks just up for the theater. Consequently, one quiet week night I was alone in the dining room except for one English lady seated on the opposite side of the cavernous room.

Each of us had her own waiter and each of us gradually became aware that there seemed to be an almost competition as to which waiter could bestow the most service and attention on his particular patron. When we reached the dessert course my waiter suggested that I try the chef's special for the evening, peach Melba. I concurred and noted that, at the same time, the other waiter was pushing through the swinging door directly behind my waiter. Then in the stifling quiet that always sits on every middle-class English dining room, an uproar began in the kitchen. It sounded almost as if the bombs were falling again. Great slams and bangs and thuds against the thin walls and once or twice the swinging doors swung but no one came through them. My distant dining companion and I exchanged worried glances until eventually, very eventually, my waiter emerged, dickey shirt front hanging out over the top of his trousers, jacket pulled sideways and prominent evidence of a shiner with a good start. But he was bearing triumphantly what had definitely been the last peach Melba. I glanced over at the other lady but she had, meanwhile, risen gracefully and then, turning to me before she departed, gave me that universal handshake-over-the-head symbol of a sportsman's victory. So unexpected, so funny and so absolutely right, I fell apart laughing. I found out later from my dilapidated defender that she was the sister of England's top jockey and that, like himself, the other waiter was also a horse lover. So that last peach Melba, the one and only peach Melba, represented either a tip on the horses or a tip for the horses and, to a betting man, a trophy worth fighting for. Too bad Elmo missed the fun.

Mexico

Two weeks went by before I could book passage on another ship back to America. So Lorraine got her taste of luxurious living aboard the ocean liner New Amsterdam. *She also knew the joy of holding my hand as our ship glided into New York harbor. The trip back to our California home seemed much longer than it was because we had been away for too long.*

– Elmo

Sonora, Mexico, Octobre treinte, 1955

Dear Friends, or should I say, Hola!—Mama y papa,

Como esta ustedes? Hoy in Mejico estamos muy bien!

Getting home, no sooner had we unlocked the door, dumped out the suitcases and put the first load of clothes to wash, than the phone rang. Our friend, Octavio, invited us to go on a real old-fashioned trail drive in the Yaqui mountains of Mexico. It was too good to miss especially since we had visions of filming, for our proposed western, real *corriente* longhorn cattle, armadas of real mustangs and real, honest-to-God cowboys.

Elmo had always wanted to document the real west as it is—not as Hollywood had been feeding it to the public. During one of his coffee breaks at the studio, he talked a friend into putting $50,000 up for him to film his dream. All he had to do to get my cooperation was to tell me to pack some Levis and a toothbrush.

It has gotten to the place where Elmo and I are both speaking broken English as well as smashed Spanish, but we are having a fine old time in both languages. We have been to El Rio Yaqui (the Yaqui River) and back safely and *that* is an experience I want to tell you about in person so I can wave my arms and really give out. I doubt if any gal ever roughed it rougher than I did anytime, anyplace, but it was wonderful fun and I wouldn't have missed it.

We had a long but pleasant drive from Los Angeles to Nogales and as soon as we broke out of the thick fog we had all the way to Redlands, have been in the bright sunshine ever since. Stayed at the El Portal Motel in Nogales and the owners hugged us and treated us like long lost friends. Octavio drove over and had breakfast with us Wednesday morning and he and our friend Ernesto (now the Mayor of Nogales) took us through the border customs and immigration like a cool breeze. We drove to Hermosillo while Octavio took care of business and flew down that evening.

Next day we loaded up our Plymouth and one of his "peeck-ups" with camping gear, cameras, food, a driver named Matape (Maw-taw-pay) for the peeck-up and Miguel (the cook in *The Cowboy*) to cook for us. We drove about eight hours over the most rugged roads anyone has ever seen. The only good thing about the so-called highway (really just a dirt road) from Hermosillo to

Sajuaripa is the fancy monument they erected halfway to commemorate the Presidente who made half a million dollars in graft for its construction. Many, many times we had to hop out and throw rocks out of the road and shovel in the ruts and then get behind the Plymouth and push like hell while Octavio gunned through. But we made it. The last steep climb was one that would have made a burro gulp. Elmo was driving and only made it half way up before the motor died. So he backed down to the bottom and the whole crew went to road clearing. Octavio volunteered to try it and while the rest of us went leaping for shelter (the road is only about ten feet wide) he came looping and leaping and jouncing and bouncing and fairly well FLYING up to the top. From there on not even a jeep can make it so we pulled off and camped for the night.

We were up in the top of the mountains close to nine thousand feet and did it ever get cold. Miguel cooked steaks and fried potatoes and salad and coffee and I dug out the Food for the Gods that Eunice sent along and we were living in style. I was a little nervous when I took my little flashlight (*bateria*) and went off up the road to widdle. However, if I had known then what was coming later I could have spit in a snakes eye and never missed a drop. We rolled up in our sleeping bags, Octavio, Elmo, and I on cots, the boys on the ground. We slept but kept getting colder and colder and colder, and were only too glad to rise and shiver around the fire when Miguel started his breakfast fire about three in the morning. Bacon and eggs and chili salsa and coffee and sugar rolls and we loaded up for the rest of the journey.

The son of the man who was driving the cattle, Alejandro by name, rode in and showed us an old mine road that would take us, if we could make it, to within 500 yards (he said!) of the river. Once again we made it but I will never know how. Then a long wait while everyone hollered at each other in Mexican and Alejandro rode off in various directions. We were drinking mid-morning coffee, the kind that eats the enamel off the cups, when up came the horses and the *mulas* and the burros. Also our Yaqui Indian, Enrique, who was to be general handyman.

They loaded most of the equipment on two burros and one mule but things that were especially heavy or needed careful handing Enrique carried. He took a load of two big camera cases which

I know weighed over 250 pounds, wrapped them like a pack in a heavy canvas and slung the thing over his shoulder and took off up one of the steepest mountains I ever saw on foot and barefoot. The rest of us rode horses and he beat us up and over and down to the river and was starting back for the second load when we passed. A man no larger than Elmo and much skinnier—fantastic. He worked that way for two days and stayed up all of both nights keeping the fire built up between our cots, swam the river innumerable times, built a raft for Elmo and the camera out of logs, and then swam it along in front of the cattle. For this we paid him three hundred pesos (a peso is 12¢) for four days work for him and his half-grown son and you would have thought he had won the "$64,000 Question". A small fortune. Elmo also gave him a good penknife which is a treasure down here and I gave him a carton of cigarettes to take back to his village and a giant Hershey bar for his kids and a package of Butterballs for his wife. He and I had a great time trying to talk to each other and he nicknamed me La Senora Juera (the "blonde lady"). I was the first white woman he had ever seen, so I guess I really did look like a "pale face".

It took us all of one day to get over the mountain—that 500 feet Alejandro mentioned was straight up and down—and settled into camp. Alejandro's father, a wonderful and charming man, arrived and we all rode down about a mile to where he was holding the cattle for us. He had about fifteen Indian vaqueros and they were a sight to behold. Straw hats, cowskin shoes called *tejuas*, spurs over them, ragged leather chaps (for this is fierce brush country) faded denim pants and shirts, beat-up old saddles, hand-made rawhide lariats, and the widest grins in the dirtiest faces you ever saw. We invited them to have supper with us and they all came and stayed until they saw us put to bed, except the ones who had to nighthawk the herd. Miguel dumped all the food and dishes and pots out onto the ground and went at cooking. One does not mind horsehair, ashes, cowturd, or leaves when you finally get used to it. My using a fork instead of a tortilla to scoop up my food was a source of great merriment. The folding cots had them in convulsions and when I pulled out my trusty flashlight to head for the bushes and turned it on they all gasped aloud in astonishment. I think for a minute they thought I had shot them!

But hold on...things get worse...

Next morning (4a.m.) we breakfasted, loaded the two big cameras on burros, ourselves on horses, and swam the river. Elmo worked the Mitchell and I worked the Arriflex with Matape as my assistant while we filmed the herd swimming the river. Octavio donned chaps and a big black hat to double for the hero and also to keep everyone moving properly. In a backwash of Spanish cursing and the Mexican equivalent of *yippe-ki-yay,* here they came. Elmo kept his master camera cranking almost steadily while I watched for unusual bits of action. I found a dilly. One cowboy's horse got excited and swam right on top of a big steer, the steer went under and began hoofing the horse's stomach, the horse was trying to leap off of him, the cowboy fell off and damn near drowned. I think I got most of it but we shall see! It looked beautiful to us and I hope to heaven we captured at least part of the thrill of it. Then Elmo and I moved the big camera out onto an enormous boulder on the edge of the river and almost went in trying to save the camera when a leg of the tripod slipped. We put Octavio *under* the tripod to hold it just in case it slipped again and from that "disadvantage" point he directed the close-up action of a cowboy roping a steer and horse and man being dragged into the river by the steer. First time went fine; second time the steer tried to climb up on the boulder with us and, since it was pretty crowded already, I booted him in the face while Octavio cursed and we just barely managed to convince him to pick another landing place.

You must remember everything like this that happens is accompanied by everyone screaming bloody murder in Spanish! And down here where they can make a stubbed toe or a splinter in the finger sound like a three alarm fire, you can imagine what this BEEG crisis evoked!

Loaded up in midafternoon and swam our horses back across the river. I rated a tired old black plug who got us half-way across on a sand bar and then refused to budge. I kicked his ribs in but no go! I cussed him in English and even tried my broken Spanish on him. Finally Enrique the Yaqui saw my plight and swam out and twisted his tail and that horse took off like a jet speedboat. My feet were wet clear up to my armpits but I hung on!

That night some boys rode in from Sajuaripa and said more were coming the next night. Miguel had about tirty (pardon my Spanish accent)—thirty for supper. The moon came up full and we ate beans and corn tortillas and coffee until I thought I would bust. It was a good thing for that is the last I ate until we got back to some sort of civilization. Since we had had so many guests we began to run low on food so Octavio bought a heifer for fresh meat. The next morning while Elmo and Octavio were setting up the cameras (the little one on a raft to photograph the cattle crossing from the other direction), I went back to supervise Matape and Enrique carrying the equipment down to the shore. I knew they were going to kill a cow but I never thought they'd do it smack dab in the middle of camp. I saw them drag her in and head for her with the butcher knives and I can tell you I made a fast exit. Later Elmo and Octavio said they noticed how *white* I was. I had to make at least a dozen trips back for things, but I waited until she quit bawling and I never once looked that way if I could help it. Need I tell you I stayed down at the river just as long as I could.

Finally it was time we had to go back for supper. There lay the bloody skin and hanging all over the rocks and strung on ropes between the trees were dripping hunks of meat. The entrails were in a heap about ten feet from my bed and I thought *"Old girl, if you come through this, nothing will ever faze you."* I made it, kids, but I can tell you it was touch and go with my queasy stomach from there on. Elmo tactfully suggested to Octavio that the offal be removed and I took advantage of the lull in activities to go down stream about a mile for a bath and to get away from the smell of fresh-killed cow. At that point I would have taken all the snakes and gila monsters in Sonora state for company if it meant getting out of that camp for awhile.

I took my clean clothes (one of Elmo's old shirts), towel, and soap, comb, and toothbrush and found a spot where the river curved and left about an acre of big rocks. Octavio told all the men to keep away from that area while I bathed. It was a good try. I just got stripped down to the buff and was sitting on a rock overhanging the river and washing my underpants and bra when I noticed I had company. About three feet away on another rock sat a little *picquita,* a scorpion. Across the river two big red bulls decided to liven the scene with a fight, and behind me some hundred yards came an Indian boy from the mines hunting a lost burro. What did I do? I hit the scorpion with a big rock, ignored the Indian, and watched the bullfight! How's that for poise?

When I went back to camp the very worst of the cow had been removed and I decided I would look at the strings of meat, the bloody hide, and force myself to ignore them. I did and I did. Feeling quite proud of myself I strolled over to sit on my cot and be the queen of the cow camp and *mi gawd*! What do you think was tilted up against the end of it? The severed head! I think Miguel the cook is blessed with second sight. He must have seen my knees start to buckle for he hollered, *"Senora – quire café?"* And I just barely made it over to him and drank the whole potful of strong black coffee without coming up for air.

In spite of it, when it grew dark we had a good time. One boy had brought an accordion and we all sang and everyone bedded down in a circle around the fire. I almost forgot the cow in the dark with the full moon shining and the river talking a few feet away and everyone having a big time. It was later when they scraped the coals into a heap and buried the cow's head to cook all night and be piping hot for breakfast that I crawled into my sleeping bag, zipped it up over my head and just plain stayed there until breakfast was over the next morning!

Love,
Lorraine

November, 1955

Dear Ones,

Your lesson for today: "How to Find a Wild Cow"

In the Southwest these days those curly brown, white-faced cattle you see behind fences are aristocrats. And so are their cousins the Angus, sired by blooded bulls, vaccinated and dosed with vitamins, watched and weighed, catered to with salt blocks and enriched supplemental feed, moved to or from pasturage by soft words and gentle assurance. The American public likes its beefsteak thick and tender!

But in Mexico a cow is a cow. Meat to eat and that's that. So when we wanted to plot the old time sequences for *The Cowboy*, we had to go across into Sonora to hunt for bad cattle. Range land is scarce and expensive in the arid southwest, so the cattle north of the line must be worthy of their keep. The same holds true in the northernmost sections of Sonora. But back in the hills, rumor had it, were still the *corrientes*, "the wild ones". It was a hard job to convince *señor* Octavio Elias and his partner *señor* Manuel Cuvillo, who own vast ranchos and who "cross" sixty percent of the Mexican cattle into the states, that we really wanted "*corrientes*" and not fat Herefords. After many cordial *negociaciones* and tours of inspection, we were informed, at last, that Manuel had a herd of 350 *corrientes* on their way from Sahuaripa, a hamlet high in the hills of the state of Sinaloa. So we waited—and waited. And waited. Mexicans never want to offend you by saying no and they never like being the bearers of bad tidings. So our queries were answered each day by soft words: the *corrientes* were coming. About the time Elmo's ulcers were having ulcers, we learned that it required 35 days to drive them into Hermosillo! Sahuaripa is a mountainous area and the steers were driven out of the hills, "helped" off a thirty-five to fifty-foot embankment and forced to swim a swift river (twelve of the herd drowned) then pushed down into the valleys and started on the long arid drive into Sonora state. The *vaqueros* told us that for five days they went without water in one stretch. There was no stop for grazing; the steers grabbed a mouthful as they walked. At night they could either sleep or eat. The *vaqueros* were a colorful lot and exemplary of the best of our old-time cowboys. They rode the sorriest looking creatures you ever saw, *puro* mustangs or scrawny little mules. Each man had one mount, no *remudas* such as our cowboys demand. A good American cowhorse would have dropped dead the second day, but those scruffy little animals were plodding dejectedly along when we finally met up with them. The *corrientes* were just what we wanted, all horned and every color cows come, freckled, speckled, brown, black, grey, and brindle. There were some beautiful heads among them and in the lot were about twenty that got hung up in the dipping vat (the width of the dip is four feet, five inches). Spread your arms out to that dimension and you'll get some idea!

By the time they neared Hermosillo those old steers were more head than body, but after two days in the feed lot and resting they looked pretty good again. The *vaqueros* told us that they crossed a lot of rocky country and the cattle's feet got so tender they began to bleed and then the steers would lie down and simply refuse to move. They cut pieces of rawhide and tied them on the steers' feet like moccasins to keep them going. We got some beautiful trail shots with the herd strung out and plodding along. With the big "*Tejas*" hats and bandannas, we had no trouble using Mexicans for American cowboys. In this country and trailing a herd *any* man is black in the first mile...or grey, or henna-colored, depending on the dust in that area.

The rest of the Mexican stay was spent saying our thanks, loading up, and heading for that good old border. We had cleared all the equipment and had the proper assortment of letters and tourist permits, etc., but had neglected to take care of the vaccination set-up. WHOP! All three of us are still shying on the left side and nursing tender, inflamed arms.

After leaving sunny Mexico we beat it up here to New Mexico where we had started the fellows lining up the "Wild Horse" sequence, the "Rodeo" sequence, the "Cow and Coyote" bit, and several dozen scattered shots. The people in this part of the country are so wonderful you just can't fathom it. Not one hundred percent help, but one thousand percent, and maybe a little bit more. Elmo's brother, Skeeter, suggested we contact L.B. Johnson of Hatch to help us arrange for the above. By the time we got back, it was set up with all the efficiency and dispatch of Hollywood's best production managers. Horses, cowboys, gear, transportation, you-name-it, *we-have-it*! We shot yesterday and today and got some great stuff again. They rounded up about 80 head of wild horses and some twelve to fifteen new colts. We ran them every way including crazy. The horse sequence should be a dilly! The boys look great and all have grown whiskers and better hands never lived. To watch a *real* cowboy in action is a never-ending joy!

I must close but have to tell you about the coyote. We wanted a piece where the lead cowboy rides upon an old cow and her newborn calf being menaced by a coyote. Coyotes do attack and kill many fresh calves if the mother moves off for water. Nine times out of ten, though, the old cow returns and will charge the coyote and drive it off. It is something every cowman has seen but no movie has ever incorporated. We told L.B. of our wishes and he sent the boys out the day after we left for Mexico to catch a coyote. Since our original plan was to be gone ten days, they held him for us. They had an old washing machine sitting out in the yard, so they popped the coyote in there, wired an old wire car wheel over the opening and have kept him in there, well fed and watered. He can run around in one direction only and to date (due to our *corriente* delay) has been in that washing machine for *34 days*! Tomorrow we shoot the sequence. I am afraid when we let him out, he'll say nuts to the cow and take off for the hills running in tight concentric circles! But, like all the rest of the venture, we shall see.

I am so tired I can hardly see, and so full of water from the horse pond I am loggy. The cowboys made coffee today and there was three-quarters of an inch of mud in the bottom of my cup besides what was in suspension. I know I ate a pound and a half of mud today but it was so hot and so windy and so dusty and we were working so hard, I just kept dipping that tin cup in the horse pond. The fact that the horses were watering there made no difference, you just pushed them over a little bit, flicked the pollywogs out of the cup with your finger, closed your eyes and swallowed!

The weather and setting were almost unbelievably beautiful that day. Belly-high grass on a high plateau ringed with purple mountains, gorgeous sky, cumulus clouds piling up, and a stiff breeze riffling the grass. We also got some real good stuff of roping and branding in the open—at least it sure looked good from behind the camera.

Incidentally, this ranch of Manuel's is called La Noria, "the well", and was established in 1813. The enormous ranch house has buttresses and towers with rifle slits which were used to fend off the Yaqui indians. The Yaquis are the Mexican version of the North American Apaches and, according to experts, the most cruel and vicious tribe of them all. As late as 1935 the Mexican government had to send a punitive expedition against them for they had gone on rampage and killed about thirty people in this same area. Unlike the Apaches, the Yaquis had never become horsemen but runners instead. They will leave their reservation and run at a mile-consuming trot into Hermosillo (about 70 miles), buy two dollars worth of whatever they want and turn around and trot home without ever stopping. For many years, the government protected travelers by having soldiers ringing the entire reservation area. Whenever travelers drove through the military, the soldiers at that post where they entered phoned ahead to the post at the other end of the reservation with news of the travelers. If, by a reasonable time, the party didn't show at the other end, the soldiers struck out in both directions to find them. Manuel says as often as not they didn't find them and they were never seen again. In recent years the tribe got restive and in a moment of slight pique butchered three Mexican women in the most brutal ways you can imagine. The government, sensing more trouble, sent in a large military force, rounded up every Yaqui male, loaded them into cattle cars and shipped them off to Yucatan which is the southernmost outpost of Mexico. The soldiers hung around for a couple of days and then got on the train to come back, a trip which took six days. When they reached the Yaqui reservation, every brave was squatted in his own doorway, calmly smoking, and most of them had been there for four days. Octavio *swears* this is the truth!

Love,
Lorraine

California

The primitive conditions of Old Mexico took its toll on Lorraine's health. When we moved the operation back to Hollywood for post production, life was easier. But Lorraine continued working with me until the first print of Cowboy *was ready for exhibition in the theater.*

- Elmo

Lorraine Williams

November, 1955

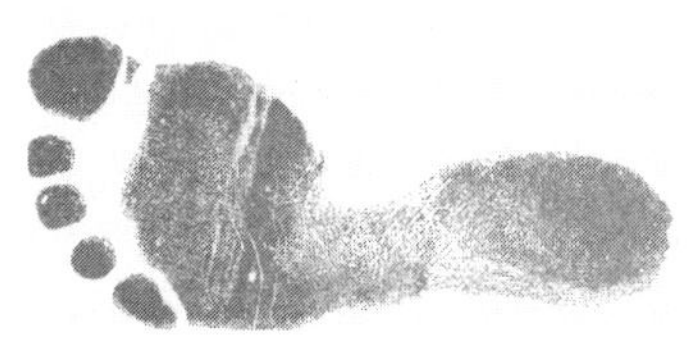

Stacy Audra Williams

Dear Ones,

Soon after our return to Hollywood, I had to have some minor surgery (probably to flush out residual coffee grounds). Anyway, our family doctor was in his mid-seventies and no longer doing surgery so he sent me to his son for whatever was needed.

I woke the day after surgery to find Doctor Chuck leaning on the end of my hospital bed with a grin wider than the mattress. "How would you like a baby daughter?" he asked. How would I like a baby daughter? How the earth would like a sun. How the sea would like its tides. How "forever" would you feel if you could cup it in your hands. That's how I would like a baby daughter!

So there she was, our Stacy, born that very morning and bringing with her a marvelous heritage of Norwegian and American Indian traditions and joy, such joy, to the hearts of parents who had waited more than sixteen years for her.

She was born November 22nd but we had to wait three weeks until she weighed five pounds before she could come home with us. That happy day coincided with the move of Snooks and Curly, Elmo's sister and brother-in-law, into their new home. On hearing why we had to leave them before we had finished helping unload their furniture, they were so excited that they insisted on a welcome party at their new address. They phoned the rest of the family to come for a surprise and all were waiting for us as we drove up carrying a basket with the newest and best ever. It was only after everyone had laughed and cried and hugged and touched and held this tiny marvel with eyes the pale grey of prairie mists and Norwegian fjords, that we finally noticed that Curly had hung every picture in the new house upside down.

Stacy is a beautiful baby and a real charmer already and we both feel especially blessed to have her. How happy we are that we can add her name to ours to wish you and yours the happiest New Year's ever.

Needless to say, ours will be!

Love,
Lorraine

December 15, 1955

Dearest Snooks and Curly,

It is eight o'clock in the morning and the world is wrapped in the hush of fog. Elmo has pulled out to get his work done early for they begin shooting on the John Hall TV shows today and he has to take some time off, as you know, this afternoon. Here I sit in my ruffled nightgown and bare feet, hair straggling down my back and the first cup of coffee beside me. And my heart is singing GLORY TO GOD IN THE HIGHEST!

Christmas comes at strange times and in funny ways, doesn't it? It came for you and Curly one summer night on the porch of May's ranch. And it has come again today in your first home and it will come to you many times in many ways. It has come to us, or will shortly, in the child we have wanted for so long. And I say *we* with a full heart now for on the sink after Elmo left was a note scribbled in pencil on a torn envelope that says, "Lorraine honey, I'll pick you up at about 1:15 here at the house. God bless you and the Baby. Elmo."

This is a wonderful day for all of us and it seems to me that I can feel the closeness of heaven in the swirling white fog. It is such a magnificent feeling that, before I had done another thing, I wanted to share it with you two and pray a prayer that the new house will encompass love and laughter and all the fullness of life for you both with enough left over to bless all who enter there.

Oh, Happy, Happy Day!

Love,
Lorraine

Lorraine Williams

June, a long time friend, collected and treasured Lorraine's letters. Unable to get Lorraine to put them into a book, she contacted an editor friend to start a dialogue with Lorraine regarding possible publication. Here is Lorraine's reply.

– Elmo

Dear Editor,

Thank you so very much for your kind offer to look over a few of my stories with an eye to publication. Need I tell you that I was thrilled beyond words to hear that you had read some of the things I had sent to our mutual friend, June. Unfortunately, I am not yet ready to publish. It won't be long, though, for I have been working assiduously (almost forgot and wrote "hard" there) to become a personality. I feel that given another month or six weeks and I should be sufficiently different to qualify for the little paragraph devoted in the front column on new writers.

The thing that is holding me up at the moment is my handwriting. You see, when I went to public school in Long Beach, they were still teaching the good old legible Palmer Method and, like the studious little grub I was, I worked hard to win those cambric tea-colored certificates.

Oh, I was a proud little nonentity when my tunnels looked like a roll of chicken wire and my fences tilted as though they would fall on their nose.

I was a slave to Miss Pritchett and her musty aroma of the stale Fleur-de-lis powder that caked the collar of her brown serge with the satin inset sleeves. By the time we advanced to Capitol Letters in 4B, I went on to win the gauntlet from Mrs. Hamilton (whom I found out years later subsisted entirely on the canned goods left over when her husband's grocery business failed the year before he had his accident). Mrs. Hamilton couldn't stand fuss. That's why she wanted her Capitols marching straight and proud and proper.

I always had to stop with the letter "P" because it looked so much like Miss Purdy, the gym teacher. If I was lucky I could sneak a glance out the classroom window and see her, between the third grade pumpkin and black cat cutouts, putting the sixth graders through their calisthenics and deep breathing. She was a great one for deep breathing, Miss Purdy.

But now, enough for the handwriting. I am trying assiduously to develop a new penmanship that has style.

I tried backhand all last week but like bangs and bohemianism, I had to give it up. If I have to be different, I shall have to concentrate on distinctiveness rather than the aforementioned. I tried the bangs and looked exactly like a can of condensed milk. And as for becoming a bohemian, I can't break my habit of being a good housekeeper for these past twelve years. I mean to ignore the Sunday paper and leave it artistically strewed. (Mr. Williams is very good at this.) But when I come home from church I pick it up while the coffee reheats without once realizing what I'm doing.

I plan to spend an hour a day on penmanship this month and forget all about writing any more stories, since I know that my stories have possibilities and it is most important, at this stage of the game, to concentrate on being a more interesting person. My diet is coming along fine and I am exercising two hours on Monday, Wednesday, and Fridays at Peggy O'Neil's gym. I may never eat a hard-boiled egg again after I finish another two weeks on the diet, but it will be worth it if I can punch another hole with the ice pick in all my dress belts.

I thought you might be interested in knowing that I have a Siamese cat, named Tita Bagoose, who should be quite photogenic when the time comes for me to pose for the little picture that accompanies the little paragraph in the front column dedicated to new writers. I have an alley cat, too, named Throckmorton, but he only has one eye since he picked on a Model T Ford last year. I try to keep him in the background as much as I can these days and feature the Siamese, of which I notice Vogue is using a great deal with their models. But that Throckmorton. Every time we have company, he insists on dragging out that old purple catnip mouse and practicing his Summo wrestling with it. But I promise you I will shut him in the bedroom when whoever it is that interviews the new writers for that paragraph in the front column of your magazine comes.

Once again, I want to thank you for your interest in me and my stories.

Meanwhile, give my love to our mutual friend, June, if you see her. I probably won't have time to write her.

Sincerely yours,
Lorraine Williams

France

En Route to France

We must have grown up on a diet of Mexican jumping beans for I seem always to be on the move. My job is the motivator for my travels. When I signed on for Kirk Douglas's Bryna production of The Vikings *I had no idea that I'd do a stint in London, another in France, and a longer one in Germany so I sent for my backup as soon as I could. Lorraine – and now Stacy – began the adventure called "Follow Daddy". This time they caught up with me on the southwest coast of France.*

-Elmo

Lorraine Williams

Cotes du Nord, June, 1957

Allo! Allo!

When I bought that cute little pink plastic potty seat for Stacy some months ago I never dreamed that it would repose in the dramatic spots she has chosen for her periodic enthronements. How I wish you could have seen her, child of this jet age, sitting serenely on it on the BOAC transatlantic flight some 23,000 feet up, 375 miles per hour, half way across the ocean and so unconcerned that she could casually suck her bottle as she waited on the call of nature. And yesterday she even had the sense of the dramatic to call for it while we were visiting the Castle LaLatte here in lovely old Britanny. I couldn't help but wonder what the ghost of James Stuart, son of King James II, pretender to the throne of England, the Knight of Saint George (as he was called in France), who in 1715 spent six days in the tower keep of the castle waiting for the seas to abate so that he might embark for England in a vain attempt to recapture his throne, must have thought had he but lurked, grey shadow of former glory, among the shrieking winds that inhabit the circular staircases.

The trip to LaLatte seemed to culminate all the adventure and gaiety that Snooks, Elmo's sister, and Stacy and I have met with so far, for while it is the scene of Elmo's travail and labors, it was for us a giant step back into the age of legends. Situated on a slender hump of land thrusting far out into the boiling sea, it seems to glower with all the stubborn, wind-worn tenacity of the Breton farmers who have so long resisted the onslaughts of Vikings, English, usurpers of their own blood, and wayfarers of evil intent. Since 937 in the time of the Duke of Brittany, when the first stone ramparts were erected on the fearful cliff by "Goyon" (a man by the name of Alan Curled Beard), the thousand angry years have left their marks as surely as the greedy sea forever sucking at the boulders four hundred feet below the towers. In 1940 the fort was occupied by Germans together with a band of White Russian soldiers who ravaged the inside of the castle, burning the floors as well as the altar and the figures of saints in the chapel. Truly, here stands somber history, but with nasturtiums flourishing on the battlefield behind the first drawbridge and the smoke of ancient cooking fires to tell the story on the timeless stone.

Impressed as we were with the overwhelming sense of antiquity, we could not help but exult with the child that lives forever in the treehouse of the heart. At Elmo's invitation we clambered up on the giant platform being built for the massive catapult and, forgetting we were ladies grown, "ack-ack-ack'ed", machine-gunning the startled French workmen. Then Elmo, on the far side of the rigging and well out of sight of his crew, emitted his version of the Tarzan yell, sending the gulls wheeling off the cliffs in indignant surprise. It was but a minute of crazy fun before we descended again, sedate with the dignity that befits *Messieur le directoir et ses famille de trois femmes*. As you know, the reason for our being here is the imminent filming of the battle scenes for the picture *The Vikings* and, let me tell you, the imposition of Hollywood upon ancient Britanny has been both exasperating and amusing for all concerned!

The family who now owns Castle LaLatte and lives there part of each year goes around shaking its head in pure Gallic bewilderment. First of all, the drawbridges had to be rebuilt to withstand the charges of 125 Frenchmen playing Vikings who overcome 125 other Frenchmen playing Englishmen. Then when new bridges were installed, the castle wall threatened to crumble so it had to be rebuilt and reinforced with stones that matched the original in age and patina. And since the approach to the first drawbridge, along which will hurtle the giant battering ram, is so narrow that two men passing must brush elbows with eternity, it has also become important to build heavy platforms, cantilevering them out into space, to hold the cameras and crew. The present tenants of LaLatte, Messieur et Madame Jouane du Langrais and their small children, Frederic le deux et Mari Charlotte, enjoy the comforts of glass windows over the keyhole slots where once the longbowmen stood and, wonder of wonders, *une petite garage* where sleeps their little auto on the misty nights. So for the film it has again been necessary to camouflage the glass and to convert the garage with a facing of heavy hewn logs. Also, a sentry box has been built to conceal their modern chimney which for their convenience they must be able to use while in residence. Consequently it has been cleverly designed like the top of a flip-up cigarette box and what a laugh to glance up and see it sitting saucily there with its top flipped and boiling over with smoke.

Three days ago *la Madame* had planned a luncheon for some friends and decided to motor to the village for some of the apple tarts that are the specialty of her favorite patisserie. Lo and behold, the drawbridge that day had vanished (the old one out and the new one not yet installed), so Madame could but sit there in her tiny Rennault forlornly marooned within the turreted walls. Then a frantic phone call to the village and le bon postman was imposed upon to carry the box of tarts upon the handlebars of his veritable bicycle. But, *alors,* when he arrives there is but yet only a gaping jaw of death twenty feet wide and four hundred feet down. *C'est une impasse formidable!* Madame could but shout at the postman and the postman could but shout back. Then Elmo happened by to be engulfed in a flood of frantic, official, offended French. Fortunately, Madame also speaks excellent English and possesses a sense of humor as capacious as her castle kitchen. So between them she and Elmo devised a unique delivery system. He secured a twelve foot pike (which will soon be used as a prop for the picture) and to it lashed the antique brass-panned bedwarmer that hangs on the castle wall. Carefully, while a hundred French workmen watched with bated garlic breaths, he leaned out and passed the improvised carrier to madame. Gently she received it and you will be glad to know, I'm sure, that not one single tender buttery tart was disarranged. So once more in the tradition of the besieged lady of LaLatte the inhabitants were provided for and in the tradition of *le cowboy Elmo*—and the mails went through!

I shall write again of LaLatte and the incongruities of a fuzzy toy rabbit forgotten for the moment on top of the giant outdoor oven (constructed in the 16th century to heat cannonballs white-hot so that they might set fire to wooden ships besieging the harbor) or of the temporary village that will serve cast and crew of *The Vikings* as they film, the tidy row of restrooms marked "W.C." for the English, *urinoires* for the French, and ladies and gents" for us fastidious Yankees. Or I shall tell you of the prop shop with its new pine rafters already festooned with silken banners and rubber battle-axes or the crude restaurant that *la proprietresse* has transformed with empty wine bottles filled with lavender wildflowers that brazen the hills? And as Snooks and Stacy and I wander this lovely old-new land armed with our bon appetites, our pocket dictionary, and the famous little pink potty we shall wish that you could be with us. As it is, our love goes to you across the curling Atlantic redolent here in Sables d'Or of honeysuckle, fresh-baked crusty bread, and the not-too-distant barnyard. An incredible combination but typical, somehow, of *la belle France* as we have met her.

Au revoir!

Love,
Lorraine

Germany

Lorraine Williams

Munich, Germany, August 23, 1958

Dear Family,

Time can be measured by teaspoonfuls or by tidal waves. This past year and a half our time has fallen into both of those descriptions and has been about as regulated as an electric mixer full of ping pong balls. Perhaps that is why the letter-writing habit, at least from this end of the line, has been so poorly. Our time got dumped out of sand buckets in France, mixed in with film spools and snow balls in Germany and blown by swift winds across the fair English countryside. It was let out with Stacy's hems and melted with countless ice cream cones. We are disorganized we know, and most times we love it!

But now that we are settled into a small apartment in Munich we find on unpacking all our crumpled clothes and legless dolls that we have found our conscience again as well. Granted that it is covered with ragged travel stickers, wadded up from being stuffed into suitcase corners, smelling slightly of cleaning fluid, vitamin drops, and spilled nail polish but it is still with us, bless its little rain-spotted, sun-dried weary heart! It has been standing in the corner of our minds like a stray dog wagging its tail hopefully at one end and gazing at us from big sad eyes at the other end. So, since we can no longer live with such a sorry sprite we hope you will accept this delayed and mimeographed news letter which will recount briefly what we have done with the last eighteen months and what they have done to us.

The reason we are here is because Elmo came to direct second unit and edit the film *The Vikings*. But, truly, the fact is we had always wanted to go to a little German town named Dinkelsbühl and eat *schneckennoodels* and find out if a thunder storm in the Austrian Alps is more exciting than a thunder storm in the Floridas mountains of New Mexico, and row a boat across a pea-green lake to see where the church bells came from, and find out if they really test the May beer by pouring it onto a wooden bench and sitting in it until their leather britches stick tight. We have!—it is!—we did!—and they do! So *The Vikings* have our eternal gratitude that they made all these and many more exciting things possible.

Our first stay was in Brittainy, that salt-grass, grey-rocked, stubborn shoulder of France, where Elmo directed all the battle scenes for the picture to the utter astonishment of a very wonderful old castle, named Fort LaLatte, which had withstood centuries of invasions, wars, pestilences, and neglect. But if the castle thought it was getting the Technicolor widescreen run-around, it should have stood in Elmo's busy shoes. He had to build a complete village to house a crew that included seven nationalities, eleven languages, and what seemed like forty-three simultaneous, overlapping, never-ending controversies. He had to keep track of costumes, fur leggings, rubber battle axes, papier-mâché boulders, bottles of artificial blood, compressors, generators, wigs and hair for the chests, cameras and sound equipment, battle flags, first aid kits, farm carts, artificial cabbages, a herd of sheep, color tests, two hundred pair of black tennis shoes painted with chain mail design, *Life* magazine photographers, Viking shields and helmets that looked like upside-down saucepans, a catapult, a break-away-draw-bridge, some three hundred assorted people with temperaments to match and a very large, very cantankerous battering ram that ended up having to have a stand-in. He kept his film dailies in the castle dungeon and locked the equipment overnight into the chapel where 14th Century wooden saints stared down unbelievingly at bikini clad workmen. He had to cajole Frenchmen into playing Englishmen and Englishmen into playing Vikings to say nothing of cajoling French lobsters into playing Norwegian crabs.

And, with the perversity that is always faithful to one's sincerest efforts, the wind blew the flags the wrong way, the tide turned tail and left the castle high and dry, the battering ram could be counted on to either behave like a gull feather or an inanimate hippo wallowing in the mud. By the time the crew was set up for a shot, the cast would be gone off over the hills idly shooting prop arrows into the sea or hiding their red wine bottles in the thickets. Swords flew off handles, cameras buckled film, girl friends climbed the fences, tourists rented motor boats, the rain forgot the sun was supposed to be shining, and the wind blew so hard that men had to be roped together lest they be blown off the drawbridges into the smiling sea four hundred feet below. Along came the Asiatic flu to rewrite the shooting schedule and, one day, the members of the company that were still on their feet suddenly doubled up with fish poisoning. But in the background, sheep were shorn, apple trees blossomed, lovers walked the ancient lanes, and rumor reached us that Paris was still Paris, France was still France, and that life was still life—at least to the rest of the world.

But eventually it was all on film and the last member of the company had been waved off at the airport, the last argument over hotel bills settled, the last stalled truck started, the last orange peel rinds off the cliffs, the village pulled down, the castle restored, and the battering ram left sulking under the oak trees (what else can you do with a second-hand battering ram?), and La belle France was left again to her peaceful cycle of new governments, money scandals, and those ever-loving tourists.

We flew to Munich in August so that Elmo could get to work! When he first confronted those stacks of film cans, he swore they were higher than the mountains of Norway that the first company had spent three months filming. Soon miniatures of the French and Norwegian locales were built on the sound stages of Bavaria Film Kunst and the lives and lusts of 10th century Norsemen were played out to the smell of good German coffee, the accompaniment of weekly Toto Lotto bets, and to the never-ending whir of Elmo's movieola. By October we were the last of the Vikings for shooting had ended and everyone gone home and it was all in the laps of the Norse gods, the film bins of three cutting rooms, and Elmo's capable hands.

Love,
Lorraine

Munich, Germany, September, 1957

Gruss Gott,

The Sandbox Berlitz

Yesterday was a fine grey nip-on-the-nose morning and definitely not a day to stay inside the confines of a hotel room, especially with an energetic and restless not-quite-two-year-old daughter. So I wiggled her into her collapsible pushcart and checked the contents of my commodious heavy-duty purse. Let's see, a wallet and lipstick for me (economics and vanity go with you everywhere), and for small Stacy the important things—a small red plastic sand bucket, a bent spoon found in a sandbox in Paris, a small plastic mold shaped like a fish, the bottom half of a plastic Easter egg (the top of which got stepped on by Daddy), one medium-sized rubber ball *and* a complete change of clothes for Stacy *just in case* (sometimes public restrooms are just *too* elusive). Oh, and at the last moment, I picked up my brand new pocket dictionary (German-English, English-German) and tucked it into my coat pocket. Then off we went hunting for a space of green grass and, hopefully, sandboxes and, if possible, a piece of sky *not* city full of tall, crowding buildings.

The spire of a Cathedral is our beacon for we understand there is a park near it. And sure enough, we found ten wide acres of late summer meadow grass being industriously mowed in a far corner by a flock of city-owned sheep, watched over by a city-owner sheepherder, assisted by a furry black dog who belonged to himself alone. A barren midway of skeleton buildings and lonely asphalt rack down the middle waiting for the glamour of colored lights, beer suds and the oomp-pah-pah bands of the coming Octoberfest.

But look! Over in one corner, small smudges of vivid color on a piece of grey. A harder look reveals a background frieze of mamas and buggies nearby. So! It must be the sandbox crowd.

By the time we reach it with thirty-seven stops to inspect fallen leaves, nineteen assorted rocks to be picked up, held a minute and discarded, three fall-downs (but with only one small cry), the morning-nap crowd has dispersed. There is only one party left, a young German mother sitting on a bench reading a newspaper. Beside her sit two boys, each wistfully holding the string of a small wooden pull train and eyeing our approach. "Just Four", the elder, is all sturdy man-child with the complexion of an angel, cornflower eyes, and a cap—literally a cap—of golden springy ringlets. "Little Two" is a smaller edition except for finer spun gold hair that sheaths his head like a princeling's helmet. Solemn and shy, they stare at us, and, fascinated, we stare back. I was admiring the boys but small Stacy, I fear, was admiring the toy trains.

So, to prevent her from accomplishing the bald-faced stealing that is the trademark of not-quite-two, I quickly diverted her to the sandbox and to making "sand cakies". As soon as she had squatted into that absorbing work, I sat on the wide board around the sandbox and opened my dictionary. After all, in two weeks in a new country I had only learned to count to twenty, absorb the nouns of water flea (don't ask me why) and doughnuts and was now struggling mightily with the God-awful mouthful that meant excuse me, *"en shool igen zee bittay"*. After all, we did bark a few shins with that pushcart trying to maneuver through crowded downtown, hotel-row streets.

As I studied the "Most useful phrases for travelers", I became aware of someone or something circling the sandbox. I looked up and saw a new boy—my kind of boy—with skinned knees and those leather shorts called *lederhosen* and a wrassled-in sweater and two bright eyes that would shame a magpie. Taking a deep breath to overcome strange-language stage fright, I ventured, *"Gruss Gott"* which translates "Greet God" but is the traditional Bavarian greeting. And in the fraction of a second that it takes for a grubby boy to steal my heart, he smiled and answered. He had been perambulating around the sandbox on a battered wooden skooter but it was then tiptilted up against a bench and he was inside, deftly borrowing some of Stacy's toys and showing her how to make "sandcakies" *his* way—and chattering away in German. I sat there, nodding, and now and then murmuring *"Yah"* at appropriate pauses (I hoped) without the *least idea* of what he was saying.

Finally, having given small Stacy a long line of sandcakies to be wantonly demolished, he came to sit beside me and go into conversation at greater length. *Then* I was forced to phonetically read one of those maddening phrases from the book, *"Ich bin Amerikanerin und ich nicht spreche die Deutsch."* He gave me an understanding—nay, commiserating, look and, slowing down a bit, *kept right on talking.* (Now, this is the maddening thing about kids! They understand that you don't understand their language. But they don't *really* understand that you don't understand it!)

If I had said that to an adult, end of conversation. But a child? Of such is not only the kingdom of heaven but the sovereignty of sandboxes!

So I had to try to talk to him. And there I sat with no more than a dozen words in his language and those tasting like a mouthful of thumbtacks. His name, I think, was Walter and he was *"neun"*—I knew that for nine. And he was a talker and an asker of questions. I managed to convey that my husband and I and small Stacy were here to stay and work for six months. *"Ja, das ist gut,"* said my small teacher, *"Munchen ist der grosser Stadt in die Welt under wunderbares."* And he grinned and cartwheeled his arms to include all of his city—the new jerry-built buildings, the bombed-out ones and the spire of the venerable old cathedral with scaffolding still bracing up its clock tower.

Then, having divested himself of the emotions all young boys have: their home is best, their mother prettiest, their father (if he was lucky enough to still have one after the wickedness of war) the strongest—Walter went ploughing back into the sandbox to reconstruct that line of smushed-up sandcakies.

This gave the other two, "Just Four" and "Little Two", the courage to come over, little trains dragging behind them. I smiled internationally, and into the sandbox they climbed. "Just Four" went to join Walter and Stacy but "Little Two" sat down, leaning-close to me. Then, knowing I could never manage babytalk in German, I reached for the bent spoon and little fish mold and put them in his hand. After three fairly good fishcakies, he looked up at me with great seriousness and asked "*Fisch*?" and I answered "*Yah,* fish." Then the sweet and sad baritone bells of the cathedral began to chime twelve and we all sat still to listen. It was time for lunch and a nap for Stacy but we were all having such fun.

Even "Little Two" had left me to romp and shout and do elaborate fall-downs with the others while they towed the wooden trains around the sandbox with reckless abandon. I wanted to be part of the game too so I began quickly thumbing through the dictionary to gain re-entry. Train – *der zug.* As Walter raced past, I pointed and said it and he jumped into my game with both feet finding a big mud puddle. "*madchen,*" he shouted, pointing at Stacy. "Girl," I shouted back. "*junge,*" and he thumped his bony chest. "Boy" I told him. "*Zwei Junge,*" he said, pointing at himself and "Little Two". "Two boys," I countered, and our language went on to learn that ball is *ball* and tree is *baum* and sand is *sand* and box is *schactel* and church is *Kirche* and life is wonderful – and also *wunderbar.*

When it was time to say goodbye and *auf wiedersehn,* I felt the need to say to three part-time sons a little of what was in my heart. I fluffed the golden caplets atop the heads of "Just Four" and "Little Two" and they fled to the security of the bench and their real mother. But Walter, my small knight of scruffy armor, held out his hand with regal poise. As I took it, I tried to explain, "I'm afraid, my friend, *ich bin ein dumbkopf!*"

Then he looked straight and clean and hard into my face and answered, *"Nein, gnadiche Frau, Sie sind wunderschon!"*

And I felt "beautiful" while the grey day wind dried the tears from my eyes.

On the long walk back to the hotel, I wrote a poem:

I see ahead ... a cathedral
Shattered stones that held aloft a cross
And I wondered who can ever win a war
When children are the loss?

Men build again and work goes on
Economics ignore the dawn
The church will be repaired in time
To hear the waiting poet's rhyme

Wise men will talk and who will heed them
While banners flutter high?
More children lost? And who will need them?
Just the world—the world and I!

Love,
Lorraine

December, 1958

Dearest Friends,

The wheel of winter turns and the cotton clouds of summer, grown sullen, have crowded into the back corners of the sky. Trees that such a short time ago flung golden arms to the passing sky now lurch forlornly across the black and white meadows.

Frost tries the windows and fingers your face while the shrill wind skates through the city and shakes the houses. Snow likes to play games over her at least, for it seems to come in the night so that when you wake up and look out your bedroom window, it is suddenly like a world inside a marshmallow. Everything seems soft and sweet and the sharp noises of the city are dulled so that you can hear the church bells' murmured surprise. The ice cream parlors have folded their umbrellas and stacked their sidewalk chairs; the one around the corner is trying to sell imported Persian rugs to pay the winter rent. Sturdy Bavarians grow a little fatter every day as they add yet another layer of clothing underneath while Americans seem to shrink inside their milium linings like pale turtles in a frozen world. The same people who, on an ordinary day, would bump you aside seemed charmed by the snow and stop to tip their hats and talk a minute. Down the street a little black puppy furrows the snowy sidewalk with his nose and, from all sides, you hear people laughing. The girl in the grocery store impulsively carries a bottle of Steinhager out to the old men who sweep the snow from the streetcar tracks and stands swinging her arms while they tease her about looking around for younger sweethearts than they. The old lady at the flower barrow has to take off three pairs of mended-over-mended wool mitts to make change for you and bundle the teacup size bunch of blossoms into four thicknesses of newspaper. When you unwrap them at home you wonder from what sequestered corner of the greenhouses, now filled with winter lettuce and tomatoes at fantastic prices, they came, bright buttons of color in this black and white world.

In summer beer is the King of Bavaria. In winter I think cabbage is Queen. Its lingering smell, weiskraut, rotkraut, weinkraut simmered with chunks of good bacon, rides up and down in the elevators with you.

Street gangs labor on through the coldest days, but invariably with a rigged-up shelter of old crates and gunny sacks under which they can keep a coal fire blazing in a dented can and a blackened coffee pot simmering. Now and then I have seen the postman invited for a cup but, always, the chimney sweeps are so honored for they bring good luck to the superstitious, for touching one without his knowing it will surely make your money double before payday.

It is truly an exciting adventure to live in an old European town at any season and eavesdrop on a way of life so different from the one you've known, but somehow I think wintertime is the best. The old, old city becomes timeless under the snow, frosted over the countless layers of dirt and war and even progress. There is a medieval quality to the silhouettes of buildings and landscapes and even the people. That group of black-bundled grandmothers watching the toddlers feed bread scraps to the cartwheeling pigeons could be now or a hundred years ago or, please God!, forever.

We have planned a rather special, or certainly a different kind of Christmas this year. Our gifts, except that long awaited little red car for Stacy, will go to poor families here in Munich. There are still so many pinched by hunger and huddled in cold ugly rooms. Children without fathers, mothers laboring at the cruelest labor to hold family together, and bewildered old people with families erased by war; our gifts of soap, toys, shawls, and boxes of food can be but a mere token of our gratitude for all the good things in our lives.

Our holiday week will be spent in the little village of Kirchberg am Tirol, in Austria. Our friends, the Groderers, have at long last completed their own pension, the one they worked and dreamed and saved for for so long. I'm sure as sure there will be a little pine tree of jubilation high atop a ridgepole. We have promised to bring down the makings for an American Christmas dinner and, if Anna's wood-stove will cooperate, we hope to do our country's traditions full justice. For New Year's Anna will cook for us the German foods—roast goose and red cabbage and potato dumplings. Our Christmas tree will come from the mountain forest and we shall festoon it together with cranberries and popcorn strings and gilded walnuts. Then at daybreak Christmas morning we shall light the hundreds of little white candles for Stacy's delight.

A farmer has promised us that he will repair his old horse-drawn sleigh and mend the jingle bell harness so we can have some frosty rides up and down the valleys. The snow, they promise us, will be almost as high as the second story windows so the children can slide off the steep roof slopes into the feathery drifts. Skiers will be tick-tack-toe marking the higher slopes. Elmo and I say we will try to learn but I am sure where we have been there will be three marks—two for the skis and a broad one in the middle where we bottomed down.

We are thinking about making doughnuts and hot buttered popcorn to go with the holiday punch made with spiced red wine, oranges and lemons, and with a sugar loaf soaked in rum melting into it. No doubt about sundown the yodelers will gather in the kitchen and the guitar with the knot of ribbons streaming from it passed from hand to hand.

Christmas Eve, if the children can keep awake, we shall all bundle up and trudge around the corner and up the hill to the gothic shouldered church for Midnight Mass. The lanterns of the farmer folks will mark their paths down from the alpine slopes to join us. Then, after church, the village band will lead us all in procession around the village as we lift our hearts and voices to sing "Silent Night, Holy Night" in the language and land of its origin.

Elmo and Stacy and I will find some quiet corner to stand alone for a few minutes, father hands, mother hands, and child hands joined in the family circle, to send our loving thoughts around the world to all of you. In the clean cold air with bright stars seeming to hang by one tip from heaven we shall pray again to that Blessed Family that we shall each and all find the strength and humility of Their true peace. In the snowy night we shall be far away and yet we shall be with you too!

Have a wonderful Christmas, wherever you are and whatever you do, and may this one, like ours, have a special joy and grace!

With much love,
The Williams Family

Stacy was the sweetest child in the world, but at age 3 she showed signs of being overly possessive of her parents, and never wanted to let us out of her sight. Lorraine and I decided we needed another child to share Stacy's life – and ours. We put the word out with friends and our wishes came back double. Jody was adopted at birth when her 19-year-old mother felt she couldn't handle the situation with her parents not knowing that she was unmarried. And Toby, also born out of wedlock, needed special medical attention unavailable at the orphanage where he had been placed. So we opened our hearts and our arms to two new kids to carry on the Williams name. Jody was three weeks old and Toby six months older. Our lullabies now had an audience of three and we loved it.

– Elmo

Three angels in nightgowns
With gold paper wings
Halos of tinsel
Suspended from strings

One with a frown
And one with a giggle
One all obsessed
By an instinct to wiggle

But they were just learning
What angels should do
And that's rather hard
When angels are new

But maybe the Angels
Who came to Christ's birth
Were also mere cherubs
Of mischief and mirth

And when they were scolded
And told to be good
Perhaps they grew restless
As small Angels would.
And I wonder if
The Heavenly Babe
Maybe smiled just a bit
At their antic parade

Then did Joseph and Mary
And all of the rest
Know by his smile
That all angels are blessed

For He was so little
He needed them there
With their lullaby voices
And soft whispered prayer

We must never forget
That in spite of its glory
Christmas is really
Just a Child's story

So whenever they sing
And whenever they pray
The Christ Child is listening
On Christmas day.

Jody Hester Williams

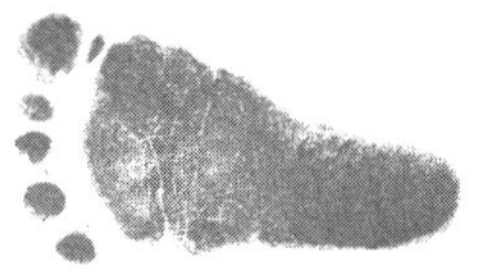

Toby Dieter Williams

December 29th, 1960

Dearest Family,

Over here at least it seems as if 1959 is going to rain itself away. Instead of leaving with a fanfare of music and laughter it looks like it will just quietly pour down the gullies and into the river and drift away into the mists. The weather has been terrible the whole last month. The air is sticky and glum and everyone cross and headachy which spreads sickness all around. We are way overdue for cold winter weather and snow. Poor Stacy with her new red skis can only practice on the carpet and she keeps looking out the window a hundred times a day. Even so I have the feeling the weather will change before long and soon I shall be writing how we have to dig our way out to the postbox. So it goes.

We were all sick before Christmas and had the doctor out so many times that I actually invited him for Christmas to save another housecall. Fortunately, by dint of a lot of penicillin, Terramyacin, vaporizers going 24 hours a day, nosedrops, and Vicks Vaporub we did all manage to be out of bed for the 25th. Elmo and Stacy had terrible colds, Jody and I had bronchitis, and old Toby hit the jackpot with bronchitis, acute tonsillitis, a rash that looked for a couple of days like measles, a sore fanny from the penicillin shots, and a fever that had Mama wringing her hands. We are all much, much better, but the head cold symptoms and coughs hang on and I wager we could set a world record for the consumption of Kleenex tissues about now. The change in the weather will be the medicine we need.

We had a wonderful Christmas even though it was a very quiet and modest one. The only turkey we could get would be over 20 pounds so we divided the eating between a roast duck and some tenderloin steaks. On the evening of the 24th we had a little party with Elmo's assistant, Stu Hirsch, and Annemarie, the maid, and a big bowl of eggnog and the roast duck and sang our carols in both Deutsch and English. Later Buddy Baer and his new German girlfriend came over and we had a nice visit with them. After the kiddies all slept, Elmo and Stu and I piled into the bus and drove to Percha, a little village, to hear our good friend, Father Max, celebrate midnight Mass. There was so much incense I thought I was going to strangle to death trying not to cough. Later we drove home singing and sneaked in the house, got the tree out of the cellar, trimmed it and put the presents underneath and had a quick cup of tea and got to bed at three-thirty. I set the alarm for six and had time to dress, make coffee and Stollen, cocoa for Stacy, and have bottles ready for the little ones. Then Elmo got up and lit all the candles on the tree and turned the switch that made the music box play and the tree revolve. I tell you the looks on the faces of three little sleeperclad kids was about the most marvelous present we ever had. I still say candles on a tree are fantastic; electric lights are fine and much more practical and a great deal safer, but for the fifteen minutes that the tree candles blaze there is no sight to compare with it! Elmo and I were overawed ourselves.

With much love,
from Lorraine, Elmo,
Stacy, Toby and Jody

Munich, Germany, February, 1961

Dear Ones,

Six weeks back in Munich to close up the cutting rooms and compile a film library, then off to Austria for vacation. We found a charming little village named Kirchberg in Tirol and a pension with a wood stove in the kitchen and feather quilts three feet high. A madcap river flowed just outside and meadows full of flowers and storybook cows with bells around their necks...The sun burned our noses and the creeks ruined our shoes. Gravel roads ruined Stacy's knees and no one but us spoke a word of English. But, Oh! How good the bread and cheese tasted on a picnic table that was a mountain top high above the world. We bought strawberries in paper pokes and confetti to throw at the Saturday evening concert in the village square, and we yodeled to our heart's content in the wine cellar on a rainy night.

We found this small apartment so for a while we can enjoy the luxury of three rooms and not be living in each other's pockets. We found a sandbox in Englischer Garten and a ninety-year-old merry-go-round. We found some delightful old junk shops and bought an old wooden Christchild and a wrought-iron flower spray. We don't have an eggbeater nor enough bath towels but we have a sensational antique, miniature silver dog toothpick- holder. We don't have another job at the moment so we are watching our *pfenniings* by shopping at the street markets and barrows, but our little Volkswagen gets forty miles to the liter and summer, bless her, is still clutching a skirtful of clouds and sunshine.

Soon we shall get organized and sensible again and back into the nine-to-six-half-a-day-on-Saturday way of life. Stacy will have to brush her teeth twice a day and I will sew buttons back onto the right places. And Elmo will go to work again. But, right now, while things are so gloriously *gemutlich* with us we wanted to take time to share our fun with you. "*Gemutlich*" means relaxed, good-natured, comfortable, unbent, snug and cozy. How we wish you were here to be all of that with us.

Love,
Lorraine

France

Lorraine Williams

August 13, 1961

My very own dear darling Elmo,

You are out somewhere in the grey mists of this Paris Sunday and, as always, you are making those around you—namely Stacy Bacy, Tee Tie Toby, and Jody Doo Doo—happy with the special sort of happiness you always generate. Tired as you are, you have devoted your free day to us. I am sorry that I had the bellyache and partly loused the day up. But inspired by your many, many examples, I have worked a "cure" and am feeling back to almost par again. Of course, I don't know if it is what the doctor would have prescribed but it worked—especially the hot whiskey punch to relax me. I just get to going too hard sometimes and the motor keeps running after I've shut the gas off—or is that too close to correct for my knowledge of things mechanical? So be it; I am fine now and dinner is waiting on the stove, the apartment is clean, table is set, and instead of continuing to run to the balcony to peer down for my loved ones, I decided to write you a silly letter.

Silly because there is no reason for it nor need, but I would just like to do something nicer for you once in awhile than fold your shorts and scrub your kitchen floor. You know I was thinking last night (while the stomach cramps galloped up and down like scales on a twisted piano)...that Solvang deal, as good as it sounds, it is not for me provided you are only going to be able to make it home week-ends. After all, boy, I didn't marry you for Saturdays and Sundays and those long dry spells in between are not at all to my liking. I know—who knows better—the necessity for separations due to work and I think we both accept them gracefully. But separation for any other reason and merely for a better life for me and the kids you can stuff down the nearest gopher hole. We have gone this far together—chicken, feathers, and pheasant under glass—and by dad we are going to stay glued through the rest of it. When you can let down and move away from the celluloid life then we will all go together.

Our kids are great and one reason they are great is because they are part of us—but don't forget they are only a part. We—you and me—were the only original founders of the Semicolon Cinnamon Bun Club—and I wouldn't trade that honor for all of Paris piled on top of Munich underneath London with a Solvang fringe on top.

You buzz me, kid. You lift me up and never let me down. I go for you always and all ways. But wouldn't you think that now our marriage has come of age, I might grow up? Instead I get sort of giddy just contemplating all the good things we have accumulated and shared together and, of course, I thank God constantly for giving us the privilege. But then I think he has always favored me, certainly since that long ago night when I first met my towhead Okie Prince Charming, and for that I shall be eternally glad!!!!

Love you, honey.
Lorraine

St. Cloud, Seine et Oise, January 1, 1961

Dearest Friends,

Five years ago today we sent out cards marked with the tiny newborn footprints of our Stacy and reading, "Our cards are a little late this year..." Do you remember?

Well, we are a little late again this year, but only because the little footprints of Stacy and Toby and Jody have been so busy going so many places. We began last year in Germany, then went to London, and then home to California. Six busy weeks later Elmo returned to Europe and Lorraine and the children followed shortly after.

While he was in Africa working on the picture *The Big Gamble* and learning how to say "action, cut, and once more please" in French, the rest of the family was trying to set up housekeeping in Paris and learning how to say "butter, eggs, clothespins and how much please"—also in French. But finally toward the end of September we were reunited and after we got the shelves up in the apartment, the plumbing repaired by most ingenious means, the handles fastened securely onto the doors and the kitchen painted, we got a chance to sit down and talk—in English. One thing we agreed upon was that we would get an early start, this year, on writing our Christmas letter and taking our Christmas pictures of the children. It was just a few weeks later after our antique Provençal dining room table was delivered and the new lemon yellow carpet arrived and the philodendron in the copper pot was flourishing and the curtains went up and everything looked ready to live in for a long while that we got evicted! We remember the day very well for Elmo had just made a special trip home from the studio to bring the painted flat representing the Eiffel Tower decorated like a Christmas tree, in front of which we intended to pose the children. As a matter of fact, he encountered our landlord and landlady in the hall just ready to ring the doorbell. We all had tears in our eyes as they informed us that due to an ancient French law it was imperative that they give priority on their particular apartment to French families. So instead of writing letters or taking pictures we went apartment hunting which in Paris during the season of autumnal gloom is not only difficult but discouraging. But, due to our perennial good luck we soon found this new, modern and charmingly furnished apartment across the river and, with the kind assistance of the good husband of our good maid who owns a truck, we spent the following Sunday moving kit, carpet, kids and caboodle to St. Cloud. We didn't happen to run into Nelson Eddy singing "Maytime" to Jeannette MacDonald, but we all caught head colds and somehow the flat of the Eiffel Tower got a big hole punched in it.

No matter. The following Sunday we loaded the children and a large box of peanut brittle into the Volkswagen bus and drove to the real Eiffel Tower to take pictures. At the end of the day the kids were out of patience and we were out of peanut brittle and by the time we got home our colds were terrible to match our tempers. The resultant pictures showed it.

Meanwhile Stacy's fifth birthday rolled around and she requested only two things, a two-wheel bicycle and a party at the United Nations Nursery School which she now attends. It required two and a half hours via underground Metro, bus, and taxi to transport her and three dozen home-made, candled cupcakes to school and slightly longer to return. Meanwhile Jody's cold had gotten worse and when Elmo came home we drove her to the American Hospital where she remained three days with pneumonia.

On the day we went to fetch her home, Toby, in our absence, had run full tilt into a door and knocked himself silly and blackened both eyes. But a few days later, gazing out at the magnificent panorama of Paris under a watercolorist's sky, Lorraine pulled the dusty typewriter off the shelf and began a letter which progressed as far as, "Today the gulls are flying over Paris, which they tell us, is a prediction of cold weather..." Whereupon Jody took a tumble off the Provençal dining room table and split her eyelid open so badly that it required two stitches. Fortunately, Elmo had lovingly provided a small Renault car which made trips to school and hospital much, much faster.

Meanwhile Christmas was approaching as rapidly as it does in any language and due to the cupcakes you can guess which mother got tapped to provide the cookies for the school Christmas party. And Elmo, between trips to scout locations for the next picture and finishing up the last one, found time to make another attempt at Christmas pictures. We put make-up over the scar on Jody's eyelid and over the long red scratch on Toby's nose and over the two-wheeler bruises on Stacy's shins. We dressed them in pajamas and set up the little crèche figures to amuse them and provide foreground interest. We blew the fuses three times, shifted all the furniture, cajoled, coaxed, capered and yelled at them but we got our pictures. In every one Jody was either crying or Toby was belting Stacy a good one or Stacy was picking her nose or Jody was rump up to the camera or Stacy was belting Toby a good one or Jody was crawling off behind the curtains or...well, most of you have tried to take pictures of kids!

But we haven't given up by any means. You will get this letter and you might get a picture in it. We tried again Christmas morning just after three small tousleheads had awakened us at five which, in Paris, is very cold and very dark. But the wonder on their faces when they saw the lighted tree and the delight of Toby over his new "bacco weel" which is Tobytalk for tricycle and small Jody waving an unopened package over her head and shouting for pure roaring joy and Stacy, glancing up with those mysterious grey eyes, commenting, "God really loves us, doesn't He?" is something so full of blessedness that no camera can hope to catch it all. Only memory can retain it.

We shared Christmas Day with many delightful people, Americans, English, French, and were privileged to provide a load of coal and a box of groceries for a charming old Italian lady whose friendship, in return, was a precious gift.

Now the bright New Year has arrived. We were close to Notre Dame de Paris last night and heard her venerable bells chime midnight to tell us to be of good cheer and good faith. We exchanged "Bonne Annés" and kisses on both cheeks with those around us, the owner of the restaurant, the young waiters, the chef, the customers, and two fiercely mustachioed taxi drivers who had stopped in for a glass of wine. Then we drove amidst the happy honking throng that filled the Champs Elysées from the Place de la Concorde to the Arc de Triomphe and came home feeling that we truly belonged to Paris as well as to the many other places we have lived.

This morning we took some more pictures—of the children mixing hotcake batter and of them dressed in their new clothes posed on the stepladder. If we got a good one, we shall tuck it in with this letter. But for now and for always please know that as long as the gulls fly over Paris, our thoughts will often fly home to all of you. The heart doesn't wait for cold weather; it only needs warm and affectionate thoughts to set it journeying.

With much love,
The Williams

Germany

Lorraine Williams

Munich, August 8, 1958

Grandma

Dear Ones,

A shaky, scrawled letter arrived in the mail from Elmo's grandma today. My eyes misted over as I remembered seeing her the last time we visited…

There in her corner the carpet was worn where her feet trod the thousands of miles that pushed the rocker and remembered. Was it the first farm in Oklahoma or the last she thought about, or the shadowed faces of friends so long away, or the sons and daughters that slept beneath the markers in dusty graveyards while her Sunday flowers wilted in the unsentimental sun? Perhaps it was the flock of grandkids and their little ones that flooded out from her across the wide level land she knew to the cities with strange names and to the wars and foreign lands. They were like black water seeping down the furrows in her thirsty tomato patch.

She dipped snuff and was a mite ashamed of it and the spit can that sat beside her rocker. And on the cluttered table at her elbow, with the hoarded snapshots and bits of thread and tumble of mending, were the snuff sticks, tribute to the peach tree that struggled to grow each year only to be patiently snipped off, the twigs chewed in later years by someone's younger teeth, so she could dip them into her snuff can and pop them into the back corner of her mouth. There was one day when a wasp bumbled into the house and I watched, hidden in the kitchen, while she stunned him with the flyswatter, cut him in two with her scissors, and drowned him in the spit can with obvious satisfaction. It was always so simple to her: there were good things in this life and there were bad things. She nourished the good with every breath and drowned wasps in her spit can.

Each wedding she found a new child and each baby yet another to add to her body bourne thirteen and one raised up from another. And, oh, those patchwork quilts that always came as gifts. I wonder if she ever knew how many sunbonnet babies and tulip patches and seven pointed stars that stitched our hearts to hers.

Somewhere at home I have the last letter she wrote in her own hand and I thought then, it must be saved. Someday I shall find and unfold it and kiss her again and feel the little stubble of hairs that sprouted along her chin and know the infinite folds of the tired old body and smell again the mixture of special perfumes that old, old ladies compound—snuff and apple scraped with a paring knife, powder from the neckrim of her dress, starch from her apron, and that sweet country smell that is goodness.

For all my trying, I shall never write a letter as wonderful as one from Grandma Etter. So, Stacy, Toby and Jody, my darling children, dream of her in that heaven behind your closed eyelids and, please, ask God to bless her for the blessings she left us all.

Love,
Lorraine

Lorraine Bennett Cunningham, ready for marriage,
Hollywood, California; Wedding day for Elmo and Lorraine,
Glendale, California, December 23, 1940

Lorraine and Elmo, Disney's back lot, Los Angeles, California, 1958

Lorraine strolls with Robert Lippert, Jr. and Lloyd Bridges during the production of The Tall Texan, *New Mexico, 1953*

(Right) Lorraine with her favorite cat, Tita Bagoose,

Lorraine doing her stint for the American Red Cross, 1944; Lorraine at Malibu beach, 1940

(Top) Elmo and Lorraine at the Royal World Premiere of Those Magnificent Men in Their Flying Machines*, (left to right) Sarah Miles, Elmo and Lorraine Williams, Dorothy Kilgallen, June 3, 1965; (Middle) Elmo, Lorraine, Harry Koplan, and Sid Saylor as "Bozo", L.A, 1950; (Bottom) Lorraine with Elmo's assistant, Norman Spencer and his wife, London, 1964*

Our three angels, Los Angeles, California, 1957

(Right, bottom) Our first angel, Los Angeles, California, 1957; (left) Stacy's pink potty throne, Los Angeles, California, 1956;

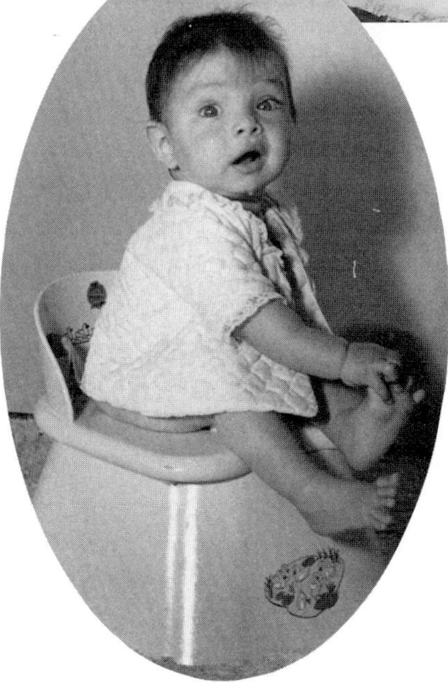

Lorraine reads Hans Christiansen Anderson stories to the local children, Solvang, California, 1954

Lorraine and Stacy on the day we adopted Toby and Jody, Pulac, Germany, 1957

Jody, Toby and Stacy baking a cake, Paris, 1960 (right); Family portrait, Elmo and (left to right, bottom) Stacy, Toby, Lorraine and Jody,

Elmo and Lorraine, Brookings, Oregon, 1980 (right)

"Bring on the future," Lorraine and Elmo, Woodland Hills, California, 1971

Lorraine accepts the "Woman of the Year Award" at Immaculate Heart College, Hollywood, 1984.

Lorraine, Oregon, 1986

Elmo and Lorraine, "Grand Marshals", Brookings, Oregon, 1999

England

Lorraine Williams

1962

Dear Friends,

In packing up to move—again!—we came across a ragged manila envelope stuffed with letters we have written from Europe, letters which many of you have loaned back to us. We regret to say we haven't yet found time to put them in book or story form but we did steal time to sit and read them over again. What a lot of places we have been! What a lot of wonderful friends we have made! What a collection of Christmas memories! Since our first away-from-home letter in London in 1954, we have been in seven cities in five different countries and said Merry Christmas in three languages. But each year along about this time our thoughts go out to roam again to all the lovely places and people so that we might gather you all together with us wherever we might be.

This year we are again in London, beautiful black and white, lavender- shadowed London. They have already strung the colored lights among the bare tree branches in Sloane Square. Shop windows in Oxford Street are filled with marionettes dancing on their strings and the collection of button-eyed children crowding up to watch are much the same as the collection of button-eyed children in front of your favorite stores. Nannies are taking proper children to visit Father Christmas and bending down to explain why there seems to be a Father Christmas in every store. The smart young college girls are home and working "temporary" in the toy departments and Woolworth's has filled the bins with plastic holly in this land of real, shiny crisp, thumb-pricking holly. The Christmas baubles are as bright as ever and our children are begging to empty trash baskets and dry the silverware to earn sixpence. They are a bit confused with St. Nicholaus, Père Noël, Santa Claus, and Father Christmas, but with childhood's unerring instinct they demand we observe the customs and rituals of each country in which we live. Each time we move, the ornaments are given away, and the toys too, but the memories we treasure, and those we do take with us.

Love,
Lorraine

February 29, 1964

Dearest Friends,

What a wonderful thing—an extra day—and what better way to spend it! I shan't waste a minute of it apologizing for being so long in writing. Suffice it to say, as Toby does, that time goes by "in a gypsy" and I will only add that our caravan must have greased wheels and a downhill run.

Have I written since we left France in September, 1962 (in a flurry of frantic last minute pleas to get extensions on Toby's and Jody's foreign passports in order to get them back into the States), or of the premiere of *The Longest Day* which finished off our last night in Paris, fittingly, with fireworks off the top of the Eiffel Tower, or of the stormy five days at sea with Stacy seasick, Jody falling out of the upper bunk onto her head, and Toby and I sliding bellywhopper across the dining salon when our chairs tipped over, or of the dock strike in New York so that we got our thirteen suitcases off only because they had identifying red yarn pompoms tied to the handles, or of only getting to see Elmo twice for a few minutes before we flew off to visit family in New Mexico, or of hearing the news flash that Elmo had been appointed head of "foreign" production just as we landed at El Paso airport? I think it was there, on the airstrip, that I started drawing the long deep breath that I haven't exhaled yet! So much has happened, so much is happening, and as for what is still ahead...

We had two too-short months in California with memorable visits with family and friends, culminated by naturalization for Toby and Jody and those precious blue United States passports to bring us back to Europe. Elmo got home for a day and a half at Thanksgiving and the two days at Christmas and then he loaded wife, children, kissy dolls, collapsible teepee, playmobile, and two jars of homemade chili sauce (which he smuggled in his overcoat pockets), onto the plane for London. The only thing we left behind were Toby's sox so he put down at London airport in bare feet in the middle of the worst blizzard in twenty years.

Elmo had already rented this fine old spacious flat from Sir Ralph Perring who, as Lord Mayor of London, was spending his year at Mansion House. Two days later Elmo was off to Spain to finish filming *Cleopatra* and we didn't see him for ten weeks which gave us time to find schools, markets, and dentists, change the 40-watt bulbs to 100-watt bulbs, get over the colds we caught playing in the snow, and learn to drink tea twice a day. We didn't have the chance to see much of Elmo the rest of that long cold winter for between his arrival and the premiere of *Cleopatra* in July he made ten more trips to New York and the continent and, I've just counted up, eleven more the second half of the year. Meanwhile, settle in we did, so comfortably, in fact, that we arranged to take over the lease on the flat since the Perrings, with family grown, were buying a smaller one. Those of you who have visited us know that it is enormous enough for some marvelous games of hide-and-seek and that there are a couple of bedrooms so big that you ought to carry a lunch in case you get lost. The dining room is as big as Victoria Station, with furniture to match, but we love it.

Now we are in the middle of painting and laying some new linoleum and carpeting and installing an automatic washer and dryer – two little treasures we haven't enjoyed for eight years – and all the stuff we accumulated in France has just arrived and Victoria Station is the depot for the dangdest collection of old carved doors, fish scrapers, brass harness bells, feather dusters, and coffee grinders you ever saw. Every time Elmo came home with another feather duster, I bought another coffee grinder so we now have four of each and don't ask us why – it just ends up terribly funny no matter how we try to rationalize it.

Soon we hope to have the flat in order and while it may not win a decorator award, it will be a home we can cherish for as long as we are here. I think the new fashionable *House and Garden* phrase for assembling a lot of weird things that don't go together is "eclectic", but it is far, far better than "apoplectic" which is what one gets living for eight years on other people's furniture with three small active kids who are very prone to bounce, romp, rough-house, race through, stumble over, fall off, and spill! We won't forget those days in Paris when the Landlord's antique chairs used to collapse when Jody entered the room.

I don't think we have ever been busier or happier in our lives. Perhaps our astute Stacy summed it up when she once said, "The harder you try the morer it goes!" Elmo's job has tremendous responsibilities, but it has lots of exciting events connected with it and we count ourselves blessed to be able to work with such friendly and charming English people. Last week at the Twentieth Century Fox party after the Royal Film Performance during which we had both been presented to His Royal Highness, the Duke of Edinburgh, Elmo asked me to dance. As we circled the floor and looked at the glamorous ladies and distinguished gentlemen, we suddenly began to giggle and Elmo put what I was thinking into words when he said, "Quite a 'do' for a Long Beach girl and a Lone Wolf boy!" And I tell you we have had many a great and good 'do' in our lives and enjoyed them all, from trail drives in the mountains of Old Mexico right through champagne at Claridges. How lucky, how fortunate we have been, and how we know it.

The children are splendid and more fun every day. Stacy came home yesterday with the Merit Medal from the American School because she had whipped that ole devil, arithmetic, at last and done almost perfect midterm tests. Toby and Jody attend kindergarten at Lady Edward's Redcliff School and look terribly smart setting off in their blazers and school caps and happy grins each morning. I say, but they are becoming British and we dare not refer to the *bawth*room anymore but call it "the lav'tree", and they have learned to "fetch things straightaway" unless it is something odious which is referred to as "simply *hoyibble*". Once Toby got mad at me and called me "a silly beast" and when I laughed he got even angrier and changed it to "The Queen of the Silly Beasts" which I must confess often fits me to a roar. Our only complaint is that the children seem to be growing up too fast and we miss having babies around the house. But, again, we find ourselves enchanted by their comments and clowning about life and thoroughly enjoying their companionship. We have a new girl, a grown-up one. Christa came to us in Paris as a Mother's Helper and I assure you, no mother was ever better helped or in more ways. When we parted in France, she went back to a sensible secretarial position in Germany but confessed it didn't measure up to the crazy antics she had shared with us. So last spring when the lonelies had got me bad, I wrote her and she came back to us so now if you want to write us in French or German as well as English, we have the girl who can cope. I might add that together we can cook in quite a few languages, swear in several more, twist through the housework and laugh at everything. Christa makes our family come out even on these cold dark London mornings; the first one up carries coffee pot and cups to the living room coffee table and we sit around and wait for the children to stagger down the hall. The first sleepy-head crawls into the lap nearest the door, the second the second, and the third cuddles with whichever grown-up is left. We call it "the waking-up time" and with all of us rushing off to different places and tasks, it is just about our nicest time of day. How good it would be if you could join us and see the mauve sun climbing up over the chimney pots that silhouette the London sky and maybe hear the clatter of horse hooves on cobblestone as a regiment of the Horse Guards ride towards the palace. We think visits are lovely so when you come to London, come to number 80, Eaton Square.

Thanks for all your Christmas cards and letters which brightened our hearts and the long front hall. We meant to write you before Christmas, we meant to write you after Christmas, but the time to put all our thoughts on paper just seemed to elude us. But today is different, a nice grey rainy spring London day, an all-stay-home-together day, so permit us to share it with all of you, the nicest people ever. God bless you all, our wonderful friends.

Love,
Lorraine

June 10, 1965

Dearest Family,

The enclosed will just give you at least *part* of the reason we haven't written for a long time. But at least this has been a very happy and successful time for Elmo in contrast to all the headaches and problems he usually has in making a film such as this! There are, of course, no screen credits to indicate that he was the guy who, first of all, had to make the decision to do this film at a cost of eleven million dollars; that he had to struggle to cast it and nursemaid a bunch of temperamental stars through months of work; that he had to bolster up a weak director; devise a lot of the stunts and trick work; and finally go into the cutting room and put the thing together right; and that even the day before the big premiere he had them rescore the music right after the intermission. In fact, his name isn't on *Those Magnificent Men in Their Flying Machines* at all, but all the people connected with it consider it a big tribute to him and his ability. And that includes me!

Now he has two more projects underway and scripts being written for yet another four. This morning's problems sent him off to work grey-faced and grim so I want you to know there is a lot more to it than shaking hands with Prince Philip and getting hugged by cute little movie stars! Incidentally, the film (*Those Magnificent Men in Their Flying Machines*) is wonderfully funny and, I must say, the audience was simply convulsed and Prince Philip laughed until the tears were dripping off his chin and he kept hammering the railing of the royal box with both fists, so when the film comes your way it is worth seeing!

What with having to conduct a Girl Scout meeting in an hour or two and having a flock of guests for dinner, I must quit now and get going. But I couldn't resist just taking these few minutes to write and send our love and best wishes along to all of you. We are all fine, kids just "glowing up" beautifully. Only old Mom is getting a few more face crinkles to show for it! Seriously, though, we are just a big, happy, ordinary, hard-working and very contented family. There are plenty of hassles and inconveniences and problems, but we somehow always manage to skid through those quickly and just remember and enjoy and appreciate and thank God for all the good and gay and wonderful things that come our way.

Take care and I promise that just as soon as I can, I will write again. There is always so much that cries to be done that I don't dare really contemplate it because my sense of guilt gets overdeveloped! I just put my head down and tackle as much of the load as I can and still find time to love my little crew a lot.

God bless you all. Write when you can for letters from home are always a real treasure and help us to forget how long we've been away from all of you.

Fondly,
Lorraine

California

Lorraine Williams

Christmas 1966

Dear Friends,

Home! Home! We're home!

The swallows' return to Capistrano this year was nothing compared to our return to California. The swirl of farewell activity, the gathering together of all we have garnered in ten busy years in Europe culminated in most exquisite pandemonium the last of June when we left London. Now rumor has it that the venerable old lady city has since sunk down to her coat collar in peace and reflective quiet since our turbulent removal.

To introduce Christa and Stacy and Toby and Jody to America, we stopped in New York to listen to the dialect, to stare and be stared at by the natives, to struggle with the funny money that adds up by tens instead of twelve's and twenty's, to goggle at the horizontal sweep of dancers on the Music Hall stage and grow giddy from the vertical rise of skyscrapers. Yes, we even visited the Statue of Liberty, but on a day so hot and humid that the dear symbolic lady was sweating more than we before we entrained to Washington, D.C. to be thrilled by the splendid impressions generated by our own capital city.

Elmo met us at the airport in Oklahoma City and drove us to his family's farm for a Fourth of July reunion with all the aunts and uncles and cousins by the dozens. What a fabulous time we had with America the beautiful and the bountiful almost overwhelming us by then. Imagine our children and their first firecrackers shot off along a creek by lingering twilight. Imagine fried catfish, smothered chicken, barbecued quail, mashed potatoes with puddles of butter, tubs of sweet corn, peaches and tomatoes blushing fat and rosy and the ranks of cakes and pies and homemade breads that spell old-fashioned hospitality. Imagine beds in rows in the cool dim farm cellar each night and grownups talking and laughing until children wakened and begged *us* to shut up and go to sleep. Imagine a clump of men almost always in the shade of the pecan trees talking and turning the handle of an ice cream freezer. And imagine women visiting in the kitchen and children rollicking in barn and trees and meadows and deeping the swimming hole pocketed with splash and shouting matches. No wonder fireflies blinked their astonishment in counterpoint. Imagine—well, imagine *happy*—for that's what it was.

Then on to California and owning our very own home for the first time in years. At last we can bang nails into walls and let our paintings laugh back at each other; we can marshal ranks of antique cookie moulds onto dining room walls and let the old court cupboard lean comfortably against fresh-painted walls. We can swim at dawn or midnight, we can cook indoors or out, we can shout and sing and disturb no one. We have settled in now, more or less. There is more to be unpacked, but less danger that if you open a cupboard you will be inundated with the results of our eclectic passionate collecting instinct. There is more inclination to sit and savor the joys of home and less desire to leave them.

Elmo's work has accelerated again until his many, many plans seem to swirl around him like dust devils around the mesas. He has been again to Europe and to the Orient finding those special places and those special people that make his films unique. His enthusiasm is as contagious as it ever was in any country, any language, or any endeavor.

Christa has acquired the Yankee way of life with her usual aplomb, driven the freeways with skill, charmed all the people at Twentieth Century Fox where she works as Elmo's secretary. She is so acclimated that even her giggle is pasteurized, homogenized and strictly Grade A American.

Stacy is true to her heritage. She braves the pool early each morning which, perhaps, contributes to her ability to continue as a top student and our most efficient helper and enchanting companion. She is still a super Junior Girl Scout and a mean recorder player as well. Her quicksilver personality is, somehow, shinier than ever.

Toby has discovered baseball but found out to his great chagrin that his softball is not so soft that it won't go through a window. His eager mind still goes questing off into fascinating fields and comes back with enough grime—and magic—to keep his grin supplied.

Jody has invented friends and neighbors as though they were waiting just for her. Her merry glances and cascading laughter follow her flying feet and tangled drift of hair into many new hearts. She is a child to rival the sun in loving warmth and spontaneity.

We keep busy—busy with families and friends and work and projects: a papier maché volcano for Third Grade, a fancy cookie bake for Scouts, some fascinating collages from torn tissue papers and glue, a romp with our ginger kitten with the question mark tail, a new garden filling up with fat cushions of marguerites and marigolds as bright and big as brass doorknobs. Just seeing and doing and talking and finding out about life with arms still flung open and days still stretched tall.

This time of year we always gather in the ribbons of friendship. People dear to us and now far away: a gentle tug from our hearts to yours so we shan't forget the wondrous sharings you have given us. The joy of being amidst others so long missed and now nearby again. Hopes for a future as rich as the past in challenges and accomplishments, in a manner overspilling with all that is good and worthwhile. Life *is* such a privilege in itself and our lives have been frosted with so many layers of happiness that we wish we could send great slices of it to each of you. But, alas, sentiment is easier to mail, so please accept, herewith, all the fond and affectionate good wishes from a family noted for its wishabilities.

We send our loving thoughts to you for a truly blessed Christmas and a truly new and sparkling year ahead.

The Williams

Woodland Hills, California, Christmas, 1967

Dear Family and Friends,

Digging like a frantic cocker spaniel through one of many boxes of papers piled, papers jumbled, and papers patiently waiting to be sorted, I came across a big envelope that had obviously seen almost as many voyages and packings and unpackings as I have. Since it had my name on it, I was curious so I upended it and out came spilling a tidal wave of my old letters! It wasn't what I was rummaging for—whatever that was is now forgotten—for I sat a too-long time reading again what I had written to so many of you from so many places and so many times ago. The truly heart-warming thing—and miraculous to me—is that so many of you had at one time or another sent me back some of these letters with a plea to do something about them so that they might be shared with others. I haven't done it, you know, but only because time is something I never seem to have enough of. Still, while I was engulfed in those letters, I was in the midst of a vast and beloved company and past merged with present, horizons melted, and far distances dissolved. You were all there with me with whatever laugh, or words, or kindnesses, or shared moments, in whatever country and whatever language, that made you so dear to me—then and now. The room was filled with you and many others and you gave me back, then, more than I can have ever given you!

There were letters from London in the 1950s written when the pipes froze in our little top-story flat overlooking snowy Hyde Park Gardens which I typed sitting cross-legged five inches away from a feeble electric heater, a wooly blanket like a tee-pee over my shoulders, wearing mittens. There were letters from France written when Elmo was gone to Africa and the toilet in our apartment had blown up and all three children were sick, sick, sick with dysentery and I couldn't speak a word of understandable French. I could sing it, yes, but what good is a classic repertory song like "L'heure Exquise" at a time when you need a good plumber and Kaopectate more than you need an accompanist?

There were letters written even earlier in the days when Elmo and I were on our year long stay to document the cowboys on film and accounts of baths in horse troughs and discoveries of things like baby cottontail rabbits—no more than a cupped handful of silky brown fur and puddle blue eyes. Dawns as new as creation and sunsets that are still streaked across my soul; worries as formidable as mountain ranges and hopes tumbling like cumulus clouds in front of the winds.

There were letters from Germany that sent small Stacy racing again in her red snowsuit across grassy meadows into shadowed forests, and found dumpling Jody singing baby songs to the flickering candles on the Christmas tree. There was two-year-old Toby sitting in the middle of the kitchen floor in the tin dishpan, trying desperately and doggedly to pick his own self up by lifting on the rim of the pan. There was laughter and homesickness and the struggle to communicate—to new friends and to old. There were letters from London in the 1960s when we tried to fill those vast halls of Eaton Square with paper mobiles and merriment.

There was a letter from Austria about a Christmas so enchanting that we could have pasted ourselves into a storybook. Then, too, I found the announcement of Stacy's birth and her wee footprint that told you of the best present Elmo and I ever had for she was the gift and the catalyst that made us a family. And there was the announcement of Toby and Jody—a threefold letter with three footprints—that tripled our good fortune. So much, so much! Postmarks from Normandy, from Sweden, Sonora in old Mexico, Denmark, Norway, Avignon, New York, Hollywood, Portugal and Kirchberg im Tyrol, London, Paris. Stationery that ranged from ruled tablets to backs of travel folders to paper napkins to whatever there was available that I could reach out to write on. Letters written beside sand boxes, in bus stations, waiting for cows to cross a river or babies to waken or Elmo to come home, or to shut out loneliness or simply because there was so much inside of me that was wonder-filled that I had to give some of it away. Funny old letters with wrinkles and smudges and folds so long folded they became tears. A hodgepodge I admit but such a hodgepodge. A potpourri of people and places and the belonging to them.

Now I am writing again and this time from our home that is spilling full of all the lovely things that have come to be ours: children, pets, plants and paintings, winter flowers, rocks and pots and driftwood, old furniture we wish could talk, and all those things from many lands that smile at us and tease us to remember. And, now, an envelope of old letters! I have half a mind to tie strings to them and hang them on our tree this year so you shall all stay with us through this holiday season. But, really, that isn't necessary for you are always with us to touch hearts and talk in thoughts. Friendship has this magic—always had, always will.

I thought to say this has been a busy year, but then you made me realize they have all been busy. I know, now, that each journey—be it a day, a continent, an eye blink or a lifetime—has its weight of frustrations and responsibilities and labors, but it has, too, its own particular measure of learning, of living, and love in many guises. Each year stands alone and yet they stand together. So I will try, again, to tell you of us and hope you will write and tell us of you.

With love,
Lorraine

Christmas, 1968

Dear Ones,

Elmo is working too hard but then he always is. He has more plans than ever before, more projects, and more accomplishments. I marvel at his energy, his enthusiasms, his endurance and the orchestration of his personality that can always strike the right chord to fill out and enhance the melody of the job at hand. He has traveled a great deal this past year, mainly to the Orient, and brought us home a new concept and awareness of yet another culture and way of living. Professionally, he is poised on another threshold, but I am confident that when he steps through whatever door it is, it will be with a giant step for he knows no other kind.

Stacy, just turned twelve, has entered into many new things. She completed grammar school with the triumph of a perfect report card and A-for-excellence in every subject and achievement. Now she is learning to play the flute and the piano and still devoting herself wholeheartedly to Girl Scout activities while continuing to make exceptional progress in junior high school. But even while her shiny chestnut head is bent over her books, she doesn't forget to glance up once in awhile with those great pale smoke eyes and smile that tantalizing sideways smile of hers. She has, truly, grown in humor and fantasy and persistence as tall as she has grown in grace and beauty.

Toby is our skyrocket, our roman candle of many moods and unpredictable moments. Sometimes he sputters out but only to catch fire again and shoot off, sparkling and all a-dazzle in another direction. Now he has started trumpet lessons reasoning that if Stacy is to be a flautist, he will be a "trumpest". It is a good word he invented, akin as it is to tempest. At nine his arms and legs—and mind—are reaching out, racing, grabbing, flinging aside, catching hold and testing everything to see if it will somehow belong to him or not. He is a small adventurer unto himself who sometimes harbors beside us to let us share his treasure, a most intriguing, sometimes maddening, but just-as-he-ought-to-be boy.

Jody has flourished like a sunflower. I'm sure even Van Gogh couldn't have captured the radiant intensity of this spirit as it unfurls and keeps turning to face the brightness. Whether it is the first day she holds her new violin, or the picture of her peeling potatoes wearing a blue apron tied high under her armpits, seeing her race to keep up with the older children, or puzzling over school work, those chocolate eyes twinkle out from under her drift of tawny hair. She has a zest and a quality to her participation in life that makes you catch your breath. She is an eight-year-old funnel that scoops up everything and distills it into loveliness and pure joy to behold.

I have tried to get back to my writing this past year and, at the same time, keep all our other activities and routines in motion. I am, at this time, sort of a human jigsaw puzzle with a lot of the pieces scattered, but I keep hoping that they are all there someplace and it is only a matter of continuing effort and patience until I can fit them into the pattern I want to see emerge. Each time I put down one task, there are others waiting to be taken up. So I beg of you to understand that my seeming neglect of you is not intentional, but only because I am one when I would be many, that I am small when I would be big, and that there is so much I want to do if I can.

I send you love. I send you courage for your tasks. I send you happiness remembered and happiness ahead. I send you greetings from all of us and, especially, do I send my gratitude this year that you are you and yet, again and always, a part of me.

Love,
Lorraine

Christmas, 1969

Dear Family and Friends,

The sweet confusion of Christmas is come again. All the ingredients for fruit cakes surround me, a sleek black cat sleeps in the rocker under a tangle of tissue paper and lists of things to do are printed on my eyelids. I read them even when I sleep.

Still, I procrastinate. When my hands should be wrapping packages, they slowly stop as I hear the sweet curlings of Stacy's flute and I go lean in the doorway to listen. Jody comes home from school and her dancing urgency pulls me away to go visit the Christmas tree lot. "We're not buying today," she tells the vendor, "just smelling." Last Sunday Toby and I spent a happy time carving linoleum prints of wise men and an angel with a lopsided smile when we should have swept the garage. Elmo, as always, blusters about keeping it modest this year and then out-does the rest of us in an extravagant flurry.

We are a silly family, really. We string colored lights across the front of our house and then promenade down the drive to turn suddenly and see them as if it were all new and unexpected. Every night we are surprised all over again. We build a fire each morning and have our tea and coffee and chatting time as if there aren't a thousand duties locked up half an hour beyond. And the magic of Christmas surrounds us, lifts us up and away from the narrow dimensions of time and what has yet to be done. When the children aren't practicing carols for the school concerts, we keep the record player going and those lovely songs take us to visit countries and people we love. We hug Christmas to ourselves as if it had never happened before.

Oh, like everyone else we decry the commercialism and extravagance. We grow impatient sometimes and cranky and too tired out. But only because Christmas comes too fast and goes too soon. We want so much, so much from it!

All my life I was taught that it was more blessed to give than to receive but—this year—I am learning to take. Each minute, each memory must be gathered in, held close, spun out into golden threads for they are the fragments of joy I shall depend on to carry me through the rest of the year. Tableaus like pages of a well-thumbed book: Jody bringing her violin to the kitchen to play for me when it is my night to wash the supper dishes; Toby atop the tall ladder hanging ornaments on the tree, regaling us with a running commentary on his prowess as decorator; Stacy surrounded by contented cats reading fables to our little girl from across the street; firelight on faces and sleepy murmurings. It costs me but a little time to watch the kitten wash her face. And I pause but briefly as Elmo comes in from work and the shouting happy children rush out to greet him, "Daddy's home!" But these are the treasures I hang on my Christmas tree each year and take down, one by one, later, much later.

The house is perfumed with woodsmoke and good smells from my kitchen. This is the fragrance of Christmas. Conspiratorial whispers and shrieks of feigned alarm as you unexpectedly open a door, children's voices in song. These are the sounds of Christmas. To forget for a brief time the complexities of this cosmic age, the tremblors of uncertainty that rock us all from time to time—this is the need of Christmas, in all of us.

Once again this year our children and our neighbors' children will present their annual Christmas play. I am sort of Mother Factotum: I plug in and unplug the Christmas lights on cue, I provide the costumes with my blue velvet robe for Mary and shawls to be worn by the wise men. The crowns are made of gold paper. Stacy's beloved and well-traveled Mimoo doll is the Christ Child. Angels wear worn out sheets and halos of shining hair. Music is provided by the children with intense dedication and a few missed notes. The audience is invariably touched. Laughter and tears sit side by side and this is how it should be—for this is Christmas at our house. May Christmas at your house be just as blessed!

Love,
Lorraine

April, 1971

Dear Ones,

We have had a busy and productive year. Elmo has almost completed *Tora, Tora, Tora,* and it truly is a remarkable and exciting film. Almost four years of his work has gone into it so it is gladdening to know that much of his creative intensity is evident. Soon he will be involved in some new project and the rest of us will find ourselves caught up by the contagion of his vast enthusiasms. The children continue their excellent progress in school and scouts and music. We seem to be perpetually involved in all sorts of intriguing projects. Our ambitions are like kites with long, long tails but, so far, we have been lucky enough to have them all fly high and adventurously. Home is the center of most activities so no need to tell you that my attention is focused here. Next June, Stacy completes ninth grade and graduates from junior high school and Toby and Jody will complete sixth grade and graduate from elementary school. It is bound to be another busy year ahead and with many memorable things to mark it. Elmo has had so many interesting propositions to consider for his next film that it is entirely possible that we shall be moving again. But wherever we have gone we have always found the best there was and I'm confident we always will. So, since our plans are adrift in the future, we will make sure that this Christmas is one of the best ever.

Already the first cards are arriving and I feel close to each of you. We festoon your greetings in garlands all over the house and keep you close to us throughout this season when friend reaches out to friend and love encircles us all. We shall touch thoughts often, I promise.

Lorraine

Lorraine Williams

Pacific Palasades, Christmas, 1971

Dear Ones everywhere,

There was no happy Christmas letter last year. My thoughts were with you though—oh, how they were with you—even though the words I usually send could not come forth.

That summer my Mother fell ill and surgery disclosed that she had cancer. To see a good woman, so active, so strong, so dedicated to taking care of others, fail and falter is a burden beyond description. So, from the time we knew her time was short, all my attention was given to her. She left this life in peace April 5th, and now that I have adjusted to the loss of her physical presence, I know I shall have her even closer—as a part of me forever. This Christmas I have found the heritage she left me in the reservoirs of courage and in my responsibility to those who, in turn, need me.

I wrote to all of you this spring—a letter that never got mailed. For the day I wrote it, our home in the valley was sold and I had but thirty days to find us another. So off I flew, flinging positive thoughts out the car windows in every direction. Then our new house found us—called to us—claimed us for its very own. It is a gracious old house, long neglected, but patiently showing us how to restore it to beauty and giving us, in return, satisfaction and contentment commensurate with the hard work involved.

Today the Christmas tree is waiting to be trimmed, the bright felt banners hang from the walls, your cards and letters are festooned in the greenery on the stair rail, going upstairs and downstairs with us a hundred happy thoughts a day. Outside the window the old, gnarled poinsettia plant lifts green arms and scarlet blooms to the brisk wind and blue smiling sky. The cats and dog lie under the table soaking up the sun and the record player sends the voices of joy caroling through the house in many languages. And I sit here at the typewriter thinking of all of you in so many places and I am overwhelmed by a sense of your presence.

Oh, it is so good to be with you again!

This, too, has been a busy year—we seem to know no other kind. Many big events and many small, but all of them important to us, have filled our days to spilling full. To move our great collection of beloved things, to clean and refurbish this home and garden, has been my main concern. To adapt to new schools, new friends, and new routines and to hold their tired parents together has been the children's routine. To undertake and carry out the enormous burdens of his new job has been a challenge that has taken all of Elmo's patience, his unfailing humor, and his quiet steady determination to do what he believes is ultimately best.

With the announcement of his appointment as Chief of Worldwide Production for 20th Century-Fox, the children and I actually applauded and wept at the same time. For we, more than any others, know the intensity of his dedication to any job and we see many evidences of the demands of this one. So I'm sure you will forgive us a small wedge of jealousy that he must so often be away from us, as well as our tendency to sudden anger when people do not appreciate the quality of his efforts. Still, we know we share with all of you our pride in this acknowledgement of his talents and his achievements through the years. Yes, as always, the sense of joy predominates.

Three times each year another birthday makes me catch my breath. I'm sure I'm no different from any other mother—reaching backwards—reaching forwards—and yet hugging the right-now of our children with all my being. The teen years are the young tree years and we see them growing, reaching, stretching tall. Minds leaf out in myriad directions, are never static, sometimes stormy and tossed about, but always learning to stand and bend with living and always giving forth exuberance. We lean on them often.

Our Stacy has just turned sixteen, but still the tantalizing mystery lies behind those great grey eyes. She is quiet and reserved most of the time but deliciously funny when she does let go. To see her head bent in concentration over her silver flute, to watch her lift and hug a cat, to find her in the gentle dark at the old piano and listen to her music tell of deep emotions that lie hidden beneath the placid surface is to know here is truly a lovely person.

Toby, now, is pushing through the broad charcoal blurs of busy and bumptious boy with clear indications of a strong and concise personality. Brain and body function like a fine machine as he discovers himself and the joy of the discovering. Some days he is twenty feet tall! School and friends and bicycle are but temporary diversions to a mind that refuses to take ideas handed to him but has to figure them out for itself. He shouts and blusters a lot but we know it is just noise to cover the excitement, and that he is still very much Toby.

On the delicate bridge between child and woman, there walks our Jody. Hoyden one day; femme fatale the next. Nonsense! At times there are but seconds between the changes so we have learned to watch those enchanting brown eyes to see the pale horses of "what am I now" go prancing past. With emotions that will always be stage front and center, her golden brown hair is the only curtain between her intense moods and the world that spins for her alone. Friends of all ages she has in drifts and arms-ful and bunches, no doubt because she loves us all so much that we, in turn, find real beauty in the face of our many-in-one Jody.

We are very much a family still. Our projects become the children's projects and theirs become ours. We find truth and challenge and importance in so many areas. At times there are so many projects under way, so many places to go, so many things to do, explore, think about, expound, discuss, argue and even yell about that I think, for sure, we often must resemble mental confetti! The best thing—or is it the worst?—about this family is that none of us ever wants to let go of any possession, habit, custom, friend, idea or dream. Instead we just seem to keep scooping up more and more, which is no doubt what inspired Elmo's classic description, "It is so much easier for us to get into things than to get out of them!"

But all our lives we have been in them. So many places—so many friends—so much to remember. Not one day would we discard, not one burden, for from them, the good and the bad, have come our riches. Kites and clouds above the hills, a funny note pinned to a coming-in-late pillow, sleepy good morning hugs, sudden explosions of play that send us all rocketing straight up, smiles that burn away weariness like sun dissolving fog, good friends around the table, the embracing affection that continues to flow to us from you no matter how far away or how long apart—these are the rainbows that arc from yesterday to today to tomorrow.

These are the things that matter to us and for all your share in them we give you thanks and wish you many such happiness in the bright new year ahead.

With much love,
Lorraine

Christmas, 1973

Dear Ones,

How many times, how many years, dear ones, have I written that salutation and then sat back in my chair and been swept away in a compelling rush of poignant and powerful memories?

Like the leaves that today are cascading down from the great sycamore trees in our garden and freckling the grass, sometimes cartwheeling in golden clusters blown my way by the wind's caprice, sometimes descending in slow spirals that hold me momentarily captive, you come drifting into each letter, to be with me for the time it takes to touch thoughts.

The now of my life falls away as so many yesterdays come cloud-crowding back, soft pillows of reverie, tangible but intransient shapes assembling, building, pausing and then moving on to form other patterns in other places.

I've learned to count, not bead by bead, but as if the whole string of pearls had broken and, as the opalescent shimmer of so much, so suddenly, spills out, I am overwhelmed once again.

How do you go about saying all that should be said? How do you make your little genuflection to eternity? There is certainly too much to be told in one telling, so I guess it is necessary to collect, as I do, all the bits and pieces that come my way—pebbles on the path—and know that in each of them dwells the same power that keeps the sun pinned to the sky.

It is my way of bringing you all to me again and reconciling myself to the fact that some of those I love are gone from me now, except as I recall and replenish them in remembering. To hear again the voices that are stilled, you must know that a smile need not be seen to be returned and that love, though always changing, never changes.

These yearly letters have taken on an importance and an intensity I never intended them to have. Sometimes it seems as if they pour out of my fingers without my having much to do with it at all—as though it were really all of you filling me up with what you want me to say. So, once again, I sit here, humbled by your expectancy, yet exhilarated by anticipation of your answers that always come rushing back to me. It seems I give so little and get so much!

With that thought I must admit that I feel quite confident now that, one day, Elmo and the children will finally get me properly raised. Who knows? I may even eventually become a grown-up. This year I've been trying hard and, in a few ways, have almost caught up to some of them.

Stacy, having finished high school with highest honors, has stepped aside briefly from the dedication and discipline with which she pursued education, and is now doing some of the things she deserves to do. Besides savoring time and talent on her flute, unraveling the mysteries of astrology, learning to speedwrite, and reading all the tantalizing mountains of books she treasures, she has also taken me under her tutelage, including me in some of these activities and coaxing me into a few others. We have kind of a mother-daughter teeter-totter arrangement with homework of both kinds. Sometimes I give the push that provides the momentum and sometimes she does, but the best part is that we both enjoy the sharing. And I benefit enormously from having such a lovely and loving teacher.

Toby is growing big in other ways than height and weight and bear-hugs. Even though there are quite a few more bumps and grumples left between boy and man, and days when even he doesn't know which he is quite, there is still sufficient evidence that what-will-be is going to be equally as charming and challenging as what-was. The fact that he made Junior Varsity football this year and is learning to drive a car has momentarily shoved some of the other aspects of life to the far corners of his mind, but the displacement is only temporary we all know. It just takes a grin and a rough-house to remind us. Through him I have had the vicarious joy of growing up a boy, which I never got to be when I was younger. And I must say it seems to be a pretty complex way of life. When he was little and got angry, he used to say, "Look out! I think I'm going to 'splode!" And observing all the energy and uncertainties involved in his transition, I'm sort of surprised that he doesn't.

Jody, now, is indescribably Jody. My patchwork, my palette of many colors, she is predictable only in that she is unpredictable. No one season for her with four to choose from, no buttoning the coat the same way every time. She has so many talents, so many potentials that she will taste and touch and try awhile longer before gathering all her fires into one opal. But, as always, the leitmotif of love remains the motivation for all the variations she plays. More than any of us, she has the steady and remarkable gift of caring for everyone who comes her way. Though sometimes she still resents being the baby of the family, she does seem to know that, somehow, she is also the most mature in that she accepts, attunes, understands, and manages to keep the rest of us from spinning out of orbit. From the bounty of her judgment and blessed by her enchanted sense of humor, I'm learning to let life happen from my Jody.

I've saved the news about Elmo for last, not because he is least, but because he is, as he always has been, sort of the culmination of my life and letters. Even though I know he feels this past year has been frustrating and unproductive for him, I have tried to pay him back in some of the patience he has always shown me.

There are times in life when people around us close doors upon us instead of opening them and, even when we realize that the restrictions stem from their deficiencies and fears, it is still hard to accept the fact that people can say yes and mean no. He should have left Fox at the first of the year with his gold watch and good-bye but, instead, he felt that by returning to his preference of producer/director for them, he would be able to contribute even more in the way of creative and financially valuable projects than he had in his interim capacity as executive. But, it seems, a step backwards, no matter how generously it is taken, is usually not understood even when a man explains that he feels obligated to himself and his company to serve where he believes he contributes best. So now he is ready to move in new directions and with a new impetus in the coming year, and with his perpetually questing mind, his soaring enthusiasms, and his practical and honest know-how, I can hardly wait for what comes next for him. To leave without regrets is, of course, better than leaving with a sense of denouement but knowing Elmo, knowing us, what will be remembered about his years with Fox will be only the good things and there are so many of them!

Elmo continues to be the most interesting person I've ever met. You'd think that, after thirty-five years, I'd be able to say there was no more to learn, yet almost every day there is a new perceptiveness, a deeper layer of compassion, an even funnier glint of his gladness, or a different kind of strength revealed, a patina, as it were, that could only be compounded through all his busy years of living and giving full measure to us all.

Our home has been the funnel of most of our activities. We've been in it long enough to see things we've planted grow tall; the furniture has had time to settle comfortably into the carpets, and the kitchen, which was the last major target for renovating, has been tackled. By the time we finish it, it will no doubt be time to touch up the things we first painted, a nice feeling that only comes from having lived joyously and with belonging.

Sometimes I think our family is like the bears that wander through the birch forests, select one tree, and then, stretching as tall as ever they can, reach up and leave their claw mark as high upon it as they can. We've lived in so many houses—Elmo, Stacy, Toby, Jody, and me—but I think, always, we left our living marks pretty high. We know that we shall be leaving this house, too, in the future so, for right now, we are making every minute rich and full and memorable.

With the celebration of Thanksgiving Day, another holiday season begins. As always there will be the visible evidences of happiness: the pine garlands threading up the stairs with your cards and letters, Jody making gingerbread people to hang on the tree (frosting on her nose and powdered sugar smudges on her bottom from where she wiped her hands), Toby in the inevitable tangle of colored lights and dirty tennis shoes and temper which he invariably manages to straighten out somehow, Elmo coming home—sneaking in the back door to hide his gifts—or shouting in the front door, "Ho-Ho-Ho—what smells so good!" Stacy will either be stomping around feigning annoyance in order to hide the joy she feels inside or much too busy designing and printing her Christmas cards and keeping the carols going. Together we shall cook and clean and sing and play and get our Christmas puppets down to tell again the wondrous story to the dear friends coming to magnify our family circle with the special gifts of themselves. There is always so much to do and still more that we want to do...

And this letter is like that too. So much is enclosed, spanned, intended, and intensified that it cannot be directed just to one of you—and yet it is—to each one of you. Scattered as you are, like the leaves, over a vast portion of this world, differing in so many ways of customs and cultures and occupations and languages and races and religions and age, you are my bigger family. Each year I bring you all together in my thoughts and, as I write today, I find myself standing again under the arches of your love. Like my sycamore trees I bid you good morning and good night every day of my life. And I hug you many times even when you are not here to be hugged. This is my way of saying how dear you are, dear ones, to me. I know no better way.

Love,
Lorraine

Lorraine Williams

Pacific Palisades, Christmas, 1974

Dear Ones,

Yesterday I had ten minutes of waiting! Ten minutes I could have spent locked into the cube of an automobile, prisoner of the bombast of news or the blatancy of mindless music. Instead I escaped to the nearby park, a handkerchief of green grass pegged down by patient trees, persisting in the smudge of the city. With nothing to read, eat, drink, pay for, plan or worry about, I was, temporarily, an embryo inside the eggshell of contentment. I owned the sun. I commanded the clouds. The world was still out there, all around me, but we made a pact to remain apart at least briefly. I lay down on my back as I used to do when I was yet a younger child and felt my old planet move strongly and slowly beneath me. It was good to know that it was still turning even though I so often forget it is. I looked up into the sky and let my eyes go on and on into forever. And forever was still there, too, and made me realize how foolish I am to keep trying to whack it into my size pieces and stuff it into a pocket. I only had ten minutes but it was more than enough!

And so it is with my letters. So much to say and so little to say it with. I really began this letter yesterday while feeling that constant flood of sun flowing over me, aware of tendrils of wind moving in, touching, and returning to where they came from. I knew, then, all I wanted to say, was captive to the profundity of it and cradled by a sense of oneness with all of you. Most of all I was amused by my audacity in hoping my thoughts could somehow fly out in all directions and come to rest with you. Then at last I stood up, humbled and a bit frightened, knowing that today I would only have words to give when, in truth, there was so much more that I would like to share.

Fragments of these letters come your way all the time. It is a good thing that there is a high wall around our house and garden or else the men in the white coats would come with butterfly nets to catch me. For I have the habit of talking to you when you are not here to be talked to. I am always showing you the things I find: fiddlenecks curled up in the green hearts of the ferns, secret messages written by snail trails, dew diamonds caught in spiderwebs, or the ballet of leaves that matches Bach. One day we even had a garden full of knee-high rainbows when the sprinklers caught the sun napping and the hummingbirds came helicoptering in, flashing ruby and emerald, to bathe.

You sit with me on the rim of the goldfish pond listening to the papery sound of fish rising to feed, waiting for the saucy one who invariably does a joyous splashing leap. We watch suns settling down with fog, like grey shawls, draped across their shoulders. We meet in the early morning garden when the pink rose opens a petal to see if it really is time to waken. And we often trade silences near the whispering logs of the night fire until it is almost too late for bed.

Not that I don't have other things to do and do them. But it is just that little treasures keep turning up, tucked like wildflowers between the chinks and crannies of day to day and must be noticed, must be given away if they are to be kept. Tiny shards lie everywhere, waiting to be picked up and held a moment. I shall never cease to wonder that in the palm of my hand I can hold an idea, an empire or another life. At these moments the clock has no face and cannot look either right or left. Then I am free to slip behind the pillared centuries and walk in ancient paths or drift ahead to dreams still cocooned in hopings.

This season, when our home is scalloped with honeyed chrysanthemums, when the old trees are letting go of tawny leaves, is a time of reflection for me, "the lingering days" my grandmother used to call them. It is time to visit with dear friends, to harvest all the year has brought, and to unbind the heart a moment before the crisping up of winter comes. How good to pause, to straighten, stretch, and stand on the threshold of tomorrow just long enough to regret the leaving of today.

It has been a busy year just like the ones gone before. Elmo has traveled a great deal and put together a new company with an exciting capacity for film-making. He chose as its symbol the Ibex, that fabled haunting creature, whom only the fortunate can hope to glimpse as it courses, swift and agile, across distant horizons. Need I add that, to me, it is an appropriate choice as well for a man I know who has moved, undaunted and free, through so many challenging areas of his profession. Soon he will be leaving for Iran to film James Michener's classic story, *Caravans* and encompass and capture the fascination and mystique of that part of our world. The challenge, the prospects that this new venture holds forth, makes me catch my breath. Already, it seems, I can see a deep-shadowed arcade from which I know, at any moment, there will materialize new friends, new vistas, new gleanings. I have found my mirages even though I have yet to go where they are waiting.

Stacy has been busy preparing herself so that, when Elmo needs her, she will have the skills required to assist him. Day classes at Immaculate Heart College, night classes at Columbia College, she sometimes thinks she passes herself on her way to and from learning. But, always, her steady determination, her discernment, and her well-spring of enthusiasm keep her buoyant. It is as though a great surge of love keeps thrusting her ahead of it towards what she will be. I hear her flute less often these days but how much sweeter for the rareness of it.

For Toby and Jody these are the difficult years, the teetering years, the transitory ones. To want to go forward and, at the same time turn back, is not easy. Reason tells us that it is necessary to break the old mold to let the new vessel come forth, but to hesitate as the hammer is lifted is natural. As they near the end of their high school years, the uncertainties of continuing education, of life plans, of distinctive personal identities confront them. Testing us, testing themselves, the scales go up, go down, go up, go down, but, then, how else can balance be attained? That there will be, one day, a constant, a catalyst, we know. Even now we can discern the bold and beautiful lines emerging through the blurred ones. And although we can hardly bear for them to change, our children, we can hardly wait to meet them as adults.

So for each of us, the moments tremble. Hands that are full of so much must, somehow, make room for more. But we know better than to try and close a fist over all of it. For, while it is true that nothing escapes from a clenched hand, nothing can come into it either. So, as always, we shall stretch our hands out, open and inviting, to let new wonders, like migrant birds, come and rest and charm us for awhile. Even if they fly away we are confident they will return.

Thanksgiving Day Elmo and I will leave for Iran where, on my first visit, he will show me the enchantments he has already found. Toby and Jody will help Stacy celebrate her nineteenth birthday and, together, they will care for house and garden and pets until we return. Then the Christmas decorations will come up from the cellar, poinsettias will shout scarlet in the garden, the kitchen will be filled with cooking and cats curled in the rocker, the postman's coming will bring us all of you in bright colored envelopes, the tree will perfume the house and all that is dear to us will be dearer. Those of you that are here will be hugged. Those of you that are away will be missed. But in those many moments we shall all be together, as we are now in these pages, in the keeping of each other's company and caring.

With much love,
Lorraine

Christmas, 1975

Dear Ones,

Time, the rascal, has stolen another year! At least that's what I thought until I called back the seasons and learned that I was wrong—so wrong. Time has, instead, given me the world again and all the people I love in it!

I've been so many places even when I stayed home, I've done so many things that I could never count them up, even if I were clever enough to catch time by the coattails.

He gave me Iran in the blazing sun and let me find ancient Persia drowsing in the umber shadows of it. He gave me a treasure of new friends with names like velvet, some opening the gates to tomorrow, some still biding patiently in the lingering past. I walked on silken carpets one day and on history's sand the next. I went from crystal palace to earthen village and was welcomed in them both. I flew high about shouldering brown mountains and looked down on caravans still walking in from all the yesterdays. The wind had a different taste, the dust a different veil and voices spoke the same things with another tongue. I was half way round the world and yet I was at home. How good to belong.

On the way over, Elmo and I had two days in Munich and it remembered us well. It said there was a part of us that would stay there forever too. Grey buildings in grey rain. Pigeons flaunting iridescent breasts on window ledges. The clock chime in the church tower asking where we had been. Familiar turnings in cobblestone streets still holding our echoes. Morning coffee in fragile Meissen cups, bread still warm from the baker's brick oven, palest morning sun tipping gold flowers in a crystal vase. Old dreams and new touching fingers over a child's head.

On the way back I flew to Rome and the Eternal City's eternal strike was still going on. But, with a dear friend waiting on the other side of the customs barrier, no distance too far, no bags too heavy. I gave her companionship—she gave me Tuscany. We walked its sloping hills and smelled its tawny air. We broke peasant bread, drank garnets in our wine and talked the starry nights to sleep.

Then, after a flurry of phone calls and sudden shifting plans, I found Elmo again in Paris, just where he ought to be, looking out the window for me as my car drove up. We linked arms and walked the misting streets, neon splinters flashing on wet pavement, bright moon limning skies that were meant for artists and for lovers. To the café by the river with white tablecloths starched like soda crackers, the ritual of food and again the joy of good friends embracing us with laughter.

But, as our great purring plane settled like a giant dragonfly upon the vast spiderweb of Los Angeles, all we had seen and done was lost for the moment we were waiting for. Three fine young people standing at the end of the ramp. Stacy had turned nineteen while we were gone and sent us the funniest telegram ever while watching Jody bake her a midnight cake. Toby had had the audacity to grow another two inches which he always does when we aren't looking.

Home was as we had left it only better! Why do things you see every day take on a greater beauty when you go away from them for awhile? Is it a new perspective or a greater degree of awareness? They don't change—you do. You need to. The old house seemed to sigh and settle down into contentedness as we returned, the sycamore trees held out their arms, the dog and cats wrapped themselves around our ankles, our trip was complete. There and back and who can say which was the lovelier part?

Our door is high and wide. We keep a fire laid and waiting for the touch of flame. The coffee pot is always at hand. If the weather is warm, the garden is ready. If it is not, we gather in the kitchen, where I am now, with its open shelves spilling full of mementos of so many of you. There is talk and food and comings and goings. Sometimes there is shouting and the slamming of doors at each other, but that's the way a family acts and interacts when directions differ. I think it is not easy to keep five of us going all at once but then I glance down at my hands typing this and see each finger moving independently and yet joined in the common task. As our children grow older our pride in them grows apace. As we see them flowing out into the world there is a subtle transference of power and responsibility. Like the seasons, spring slips into summer, summer softens to autumn...and our cycle, too, is moving sweetly as it should.

Stacy, now twenty, went through her teen-age years hardly noticing them. She made us laugh when she said, "But I went straight from eleven to thirty." And it's true, her propensity for growth, her compulsion to know and understand, the loving burden of being the oldest, has often cost the child in the young woman. She is working now for Baja Films, assuming (as you know she would), new dimensions, new capacities with all the provocative intensity she has always had. But she's learning at last to be gentler with herself and that she has as much to teach life as it has to teach her.

Toby jumped into seventeen with his usual exuberance, went to work part time and bought himself a dazzling blue motorcycle, our Lochinvar in a crash helmet. He is getting it together but—definitely—by his own rules. He reminds me so often of a lightning bolt in a teacup and, if you think it is hard on the lightning bolt or the teacup, just consider how it must be on the boy! Whatever directions he goes, and they will be many, they will always be stamped by his independence and originality.

As for our Jody, who still resents being the tail on our kite, how could we fly without her! How can we tell her that, with her talent for living, she is so often out front: the first to buy her own new car, the first to explore new attitudes and new ventures, calling on us to catch up with her enthusiasms and instinctive perceptions. As that exquisite bone structure thrusts through her satin face and moods flicker in her tantalizing brown eyes, we feel that, as always, it is Jody who has taken the top off the sunshine bottle for the rest of us.

Still it is Elmo around whom all of us orbit. He holds us steady—he holds us lifted high—with love that cannot be measured. The child in him plays with us. The man in him cares for us. He is the golden chain on which we string our days, our dreams. When he is away this house is empty rooms full of people. When he is back, it is home again. We rush to greet him because we know that, whatever we cherish, he brings with him and more.

Now time is touching us again with tenderness, with Christmas, with a new and hopeful year blowing in on crisp winds. The tempo quickens to *vivace*, the melodies we've sung before we sing again, but with deeper joy each singing. Some of our distant loved ones are coming home for the holidays. Some of you will be far away, but as long as there is sky above and earth below, we cannot be more than a step, a thought apart. This early morning there floated in my window with the pink light of dawn the old couplet, "Make new friends but keep the old. One is silver and the other gold." I'm singing it now, dear ones, can you hear me?

For wherever you are, we are there too. With happiness, with love, with wishes flooding out from this home to you, coming cloud soft across the skies, across the years, binding us all together in belonging.

Love,
Lorraine

Christmas, 1976

Dear Ones,

I woke up so early this morning that I caught the world holding its breath! It was that tiny heartbeat between silence and sound when silence is more profound than sound. It was that eye blink between night and day when earth is luminous and sun the laggard. It was but a moment that ended the moment I found it. Too rare, too seldom, to be kept.

Some sleepy sparrow in the nests tucked into the tiles that scallop our roof nudged another sleepy sparrow and the silence was torn. The tallest of our sycamores snagged a streamer of morning and night fled.

I put on my robe and went into the garden to join the celebrants. Cats woke and curled rose petal tongues into morning yawns. Dog stretched front, stretched back and then, curious, came following. Goldfish, motionless arrows pointed east, broke and splashed as I passed the pond. And birds began their dawn chorus, explaining the miracle to me.

But I already knew that moment because I have known so many. Our lives have somersaulted merrily so long, like circus clowns holding each other's ankles, that up-and-down and side-to-side have lost their distinctions. It is, rather, the exhilarating flow of circles, each one beginning in the last one's ending, that carries us along. So I cannot define precisely just what we have done, just what we hope to do. We are all doing too much and reaching out for more.

Elmo and Stacy have just returned from New Mexico where they shot *Sidewinder One,* bringing home an exuberance of stories and a wreath of new friends. And it was when I visited them for four tawny days in Taos that I knew our Stacy had truly grown up. That, too, was one of those joyous, unexpected moments, unnoticed and unimportant to most, but yet an unmistakable turning in time. Stacy has always walked one pace behind me. If I stopped, she stopped; I could never get her to walk beside me. Something, she knew not what, always held her back that little bit. But, when she met me in New Mexico, she strode out ahead of me, luminous grey eyes smiling back, inviting me into her new world. No mother ever followed more eagerly.

With Toby we still stand astride a teeter-totter, halfway between tough and tender. Sometimes the board tilts downwards and you know you'll feel the jolt as it hits ground, other times you know he will catch the weight and thrust himself high in the air. He doesn't know any better than we do what the cadence will be for, at eighteen, he is still making friends with himself, which really doesn't leave much time for the rest of us. When he was a little boy, he used to come into our bedroom early morning and declare, "Now, I'll give you a kiss, a nibble on the ear and make my funny noise. Then you get up and fix my breakfast!" He hasn't changed much for he retains that propensity to waken you out of complacency, but he does it with such honesty, such purpose, that it refreshes you. His moment, when it comes, will surely be a remarkable one.

Jody is our golden coin spinning in the sun, never quite knowing, herself, on which side of today she is going to land. With still too many roles to play, still too much delight in keeping the rest of us guessing, she ribbons a deep seriousness about life with teasing, with mood swings, and with a fine sense of humor. The real gift of Jody, though, still lies in a box, within a box, within a box. Yet with what anticipation, what eagerness, we unfold each colorful crumple of tissue paper, knowing that, someday, we shall at last catch her magic too.

Soon Elmo and I will be flying off to Iran, to Greece, perhaps to London. Already I'm reaching out for that tomorrow even while I'm loathe to let go of today. How good, though, to have three young people urging me to go, to take time off to find new adventures, new friends, new moments. For, wherever I've gone with Elmo, I've invariably found the sunrises and the storms more vivid, more exciting. His vast capacity for living, for loving life, is contagious. And, even though he keeps me running to keep up with his enthusiasms, his many accomplishments, his dreams, I could never imagine them in any way diminished.

Today I read through a box of letters we have written each other from France, from Germany, from Portugal, from Ireland, from Africa and Japan. Each letter meant separation and loneliness with each of us reassuring the other that being apart could only make being together better. This last trip he phoned me late one night to tell me he had suddenly realized just how lucky we were, to have gone to so many places, to have shared so much, to be so very rich in family and friends. And I knew, then, that even though we are many times pulled far apart, many times too crowded together, that it didn't matter. For we shall always be, the five of us, like five silver links in the hands of Time the Magician, a family, and forever intertwined.

At Christmastime when Elmo and I come home, the rest of you will be here waiting. For this old house is packed with memories, tangible and touchable, of all those places we have lived, of all you dear friends who have shared so much with us. We open the doors to you. You walk up the stairs beside us. You will be with us in all we do this season of drawing close again. Elmo has already talked to the roses and they promise to be in full fragrant blossom. The poinsettias have set their December clocks and ivy is hugging the walls. I will hurry to get cookies and fruitcakes and rum cakes baked ahead and bring all the fat, old, stuffed Santa dolls I collect up from the cellar to supervise. Stacy has polished her silver flute and propped up the book of carols. Jody will happily open all the cards and letters and festoon them amid the evergreens on the hall railings. And Toby will do his annual battle with the colored lights, stringing them with electric abandon all over the house.

Then as we are gathering together in our home, we know you will be gathering together in yours. The fire will burn brighter, the woodsmoke smell sweeter, and contentment will come and sit quietly beside us because we are aware of gently touching that part of ourselves that is all of you. It really won't matter that time and distance crowd between us for we can dissolve them in a moment—a moment we shall find again this year—and send to you with all the love, and intensity, and the continuing happiness your friendship gives to us.

Love,
Lorraine

Lorraine Williams

Pacific Palisades, Christmas, 1977

Dear Ones,

Each season has its symbols. Spring is apple green like a new year growing and summer unfolds, fulfills, and then hesitates before nodding to the sensuous languor of autumn. But here in California winter has a way of hiding behind gossamer skirts of sunshine, still flaunting a fan of leafy trees to catch us, each year, astonished by the last page of the calendar. How loathe we are to close the book. How often we glance back across the pages, remembering the year while time so softly turns the earth beneath our feet.

But then some small magic happens to catch us up with the moment and tilt us happily into the tomorrows, arms filled with all the todays we must take with us. And today my magic came! Elmo phoned from Iran inviting Toby and me to join him and Stacy and Jody for Christmas in Austria!

Suddenly the year was crammed into a suitcase, the kitchen engulfed in snow and pine forests while anticipation and exhilaration chased each other up and down the slopes. Toby and I are wearing our smiles tied in bow knots atop our heads.

For six long months we have been a family apart. Elmo and Stacy left in June for Iran and the arduous task of filming James Michener's *Caravans.* Jody went to visit them in September and they put her caring talents to work. So Toby and I have double-timed here to keep all the home and stateside projects moving. It has been such a busy time, such a compacted time that none of us has really known how much we've missed each other—nor will know—until that very instant when the family circle is joined again. And what a circle that will be!

Nineteen years ago I wrote a Christmas letter which said in part: "Our holiday this year will be spent in the village of Kirchberg am Tyrol at the pension of our friends, the Groderers. Our Christmas tree will come from the mountain forest and we shall festoon it together with cranberries and popcorn strings and gilded walnuts."

How poignant it is to recall that night and that small family circle wreathed about with the intangible presence of all those others loved and touched by our thoughts. Some of them are gone now but waiting for us we know. Some, like Toby and Jody, like many of you reading this, had not entered and enlarged our family circle. But you are here now, to fill me again with all I am trying to say to you. How marvelous, how very magnificent it will be to find you again this Christmas Eve.

This year there will be five of us converging, touching again, lending illumination and radiance to each other, finding contentment in the coming together after the necessary being apart. This year there will be father hands and mother hands and the hands of three children grown, stretching out to encompass and include all the wonders of these past nineteen years and all the ones to come.

The New Year will find us each finishing up old tasks and beginning new ones. Elmo and Stacy will turn their attention to the post-production work on *Caravans*. Toby and Jody will be starting their college years. And I will weave in and out and around all their various activities, tucking my interests in amidst theirs. At this moment I cannot say who will be where or when. All I know is that our plans are like the seasons, moving sweetly each into the other, taking us with divine guidance into ever richer years, ever widening circles, culminating each year with a small magic that brings us all together from wherever we may be into the oneness of love.

And you will be with us again, I promise. Not as you have been in recent years here in our comfortable and welcoming old house in California, but for another reunion in Austria, under the bright stars, sanding in the snowy night with Christmas, as it should be, forever in our hearts.

Much love,
Lorraine

Lorraine Williams

Christmas, 1978

Dear Ones,

I cannot believe it's Christmas—and yet the first poinsettias are shouting across the garden that it is time for summer to gather her golden skirts and move on. The cats curl up into round black velvet pillows each night and tuck a paw over satin noses. Elmo has cleaned out the woodpile and stacked the fireplaces full. I've polished the house until it shines like a winter moon. Our collection of old rescued Santa dolls sits on the kitchen counter, each one grinning from whiskers to mutton chops. And last night Stacy and Jody found their recorders and played the first of the season's carols. Somehow those primitive wooden flute sounds are invisible garlands that link each Christmas to the next.

And there have been so many Christmases, each one declared to be the best. So many places, so many houses, so many friends and such a family to share them with that recalling festoons my mind with vignettes that are lovingly unwrapped each year, gently touched and held forth to share.

The little house in snowy Germany when we first had three small children under our tree. Solemn Stacy sitting in her little red rocking chair, grey eyes content to have us, as she used to say, "all alone together". Two-year-old Toby trudging round and round the candled tree in private, prolonged conversation with it. And laughing Jody, propped up on feather pillows in the big wicker clothesbasket, trying to catch all the world's merriment with her dimpled hands. That year I remember we had a gingerbread house and wooden bowls of oranges and apples and their fragrances mingled with the scent of frosty pine forest whenever doors were opened. Can any of us ever forget the sights and sounds and smells of Christmas?

Then in France, when the children were old enough to share in the preparations, sitting cross-legged on the floor stringing cranberry popcorn chains and standing on chairs stirring hotcake batter and singing carols in three languages. That was when they wondered who would get there first, St. Nicholaus, Pere Noël or Santa Claus.

By the time we moved to London there were school plays, cardboard crowns, and angels dressed in someone's curtains. I still have the clay plaques and smudgy finger paints they made and smuggled home. I can still visualize them in the broom closet arguing over who would get what wrapped and re-wrapped in crumpled tissue and dozens of Woolworth stickers.

Returning home after all our years in Europe, we found our American family again, grandparents, aunts and uncles, cousins galore and all those almost-relatives that belong to us too. What joy to put in one place things gathered from many places and welcome all we love to come home to us.

I think this year, being home, being together, has an extra meaning. Last year Elmo and Stacy were gone, filming *Caravans* in Iran and finishing it in Germany and England. In December, Toby and Jody and I flew to Afghanistan and then to Austria to join them for Christmas. Then I returned to Europe this summer and Elmo came home. Stacy and I drove through Germany, Austria, France, Spain, and England before she flew home and I flew to New York where Jody joined me to drive back across America. Meanwhile Toby had settled himself into a new apartment and new career. Now Jody is back at work and at college, Stacy and Elmo have readied *Caravans* for its theater openings and I have gathered up all the loose ends to knit us back into a family again.

Today Elmo is out finding the biggest, most bountiful tree he can carry and will bring it home to bedeck it with all the favorite ornaments, discovered anew with affection, looked often upon and, after the holidays, tucked away to awaken affection next year. Soon the candles will be lit, the cakes will be in the oven and loved ones at the front door. Laughter will mingle with music, joy will be more intense because it has known loneliness and Christmas will settle down gently on this gracious old house. We will, no doubt, say yet again that this Christmas was the best—and it will be! Because it includes all those other Christmases that we have shared with you and you have shared with us.

As I move through this time of busyness, I will sometimes stop and smile, knowing that a few years ago I was mistaken when I wrote that "Elmo and I can hardly bear to say goodbye to our children as children but we can hardly wait to meet them as adults."

For, you see, the best gift I will ever have is learning that this Christmas—and for all the ones to come—we shall have them as both. The three tall, beautiful young people gathered around our tree this year are but extensions—dreams come true—of the small three long ago.

And once again they will join Elmo and me in sending you our love, flowing out from the love of that Holy Family, as a talisman of certainty in a world of uncertainties, to wreathe the New Year with blessings.

Lorraine

Christmas, 1979

Dear Ones All,

I had a conversation with a blackbird the other day and learned some important things. It was in a corner of a parking lot in Century City, rimmed by cliffs of welded girders sheathed with checkerboards of blackish glass. I was waiting for Stacy, but since the day was bright sunshine and wispy-windy, I left my car to sit on a discarded block of cement on the one patch of wintergilt grass that urban progress has somehow overlooked. Immediately I was surrounded and evaluated by a flock of blackbirds that feed upon the lunch sack discards of the flocks of people who inhabit those intensely crowded buildings. When the strutted approaches and beady-eyed coaxings brought forth no food, a sudden whim sent my visitors slanting off to better scrapgrounds. But, then, one bird returned and settled down on a neighboring cement block to talk to me. Oh, it was only a silent conversation—no words were needed—as is often the case when kindred spirits meet and touch. We decided, my quiet friend and I, that it was good to find such solitude and companionship in the middle of such frantic, towering busyness. As she fluffed her crayon-brown feathers and tucked one twiggy black foot up in comfort, she informed me that it mattered not that her feathers weren't the iridescent silver black of many of her companions nor that her manner was not audacious. She was content, as was I, with what she was and what she had. We counted many things sitting there. Then when Stacy arrived, my bird and I each wheeled off to rejoin the patterns that life has ordained for us. But, for those few gentle moments, we had felt as rich as if we had owned the whole world instead of just a tiny borrowed corner of it.

Such miniscule adventures happen all the time to each of us but, alas, how seldom do we stop to accept them. We should stop to pick up at least one leaf from autumn's gold carpet, to linger on the curl of a small pink tongue when a cat yawns in the warmth of the sun, to shout at the splendor of eggs broken into a deep blue bowl, to pause for the fragrance of mint washed by the wetness of evening rain. If only we would, once in awhile, stop rushing from what we have to what we hope to have.

And today is such a day. Elmo is off playing golf, flinging himself with his inimitable boyish eagerness into the challenges of coordinating mind and body, meeting the rise and fall of grass and distance with the same full enjoyment he takes to every task. It is good to see him play. He works so hard for all of us and yet manages to flourish from that work and the blessings that spread out from him at its center. How I continue to admire his strength and patience that persist even in the most difficult of tasks, the most trying of times. More than anyone I know, he can always find a giggle in his pocket when we need one.

Having sent *Caravans* bravely on its way, he has now formed another production company with a splendid group of people from Oklahoma and is finding stories and staff to bring us yet more meaningful films. Stacy is working with him at the Gaylord offices and providing, as always, the perfect partnership to his far flung talents. She is grave when gravity is called for, delightfully merry between times, and beautiful in every way to all who know her.

This morning Toby found her reading scripts in the garden and pulled her to her feet to toss the football with him. And, as I watched dark, slim sister and tall, tousle head brother, my heart turned back to a day that small, blonde boy came to join our family and four-year-old Stacy bent down to him and said, "I think we are going to love you!" Now to see him fill this house with all he is and all he is going to be, I know she was right.

Our shining Jody is sharing a nearby apartment with two girl friends, going to college every day and working evenings. But, even with all her responsibilities, she is never too busy to share her loveliness with the rest of us. Her exuberance and joy always bring a rainbow to our days.

Thinking about my family and all the happiness they bring to my life is the best way I know to anticipate the holiday season ahead. And sharing these words with you, reaching out again to the many places you are, recalling the times we were together, adds even more meaning to the bounty of another year.

Soon we shall bring the decorations up from the cellar, hug each old Santa Claus doll I've rescued and find them places in the tree branches and open the door to the happy confusion of Christmas. Fragrance of fire, of pine, of the last of Elmo's roses will fill the air. Stacy and Jody will get out their wooden flutes and lace the rooms with carols. Toby and Elmo will untangle the colored lights and lay the fires and defy gravity to hang mistletoe from the highest beam. I will hold court in the kitchen with the cats drowsing in the rocking chair and Fawn dog trotting out to welcome guests. We say that this year we won't do as much but, as we say it, we know we will. After all it isn't what we do that is important, it is the doing it together, threading once again past to present to future and, for a brief time, belonging to all three.

Memories will string the days together like a golden chain. Memories of the old grey stone farmhouse in Normandy, where painted bravely around all four sides of the kitchen was the motto: "If you will remember to thank the Good God for all He has given you, there will not remain time to complain yourself." Memories of small children bedazzled by the splendor of a candled tree, of friends' arms held open to welcome us in many lands, of loved ones gone but called back by our hearts, of hands joined, heads bent in prayer around our table, of all that was, and is, and will be yet.

So from this home so filled with love, I send you love and a small bird, somewhere, singing for all of us.

Lorraine

Christmas, 1980

Dear Ones All,

Each year, for many years, I've known a gentle sort of terror as I sit down to write these Christmas letters. I want so much to hand you treasures and great victories. Instead, I find the gleanings of a year past to be little things, unimportant, fleeting, fragile.

And yet, this morning, in the blackness before day, I sat here in my kitchen with only one small candle challenging the dark, and was astounded at how much it sought and found and touched with instant brightness. The silhouette of a rosemary branch edged with sapphire blossoms to echo sky, a golden flame of polished brass high on a shelf, green-black fringe of bougainvillea swagging the arches of the porch outside, swaying under the first sleepy frettings of sparrows who shelter in the roof tiles. And, everywhere, the comings and goings, the givings and takings of all the yesterdays. Suddenly it all came together, like a black cat curled into a perfect satin circle, having a beginning and an end certainly, but for just a moment folded into a warm and comforting now. I was here and you were here and there was that quiet gathering moment that banishes years and erases distance and hands us, undeserved and unexpected, happiness.

Than as dawn pushed softly into this old house, it brought extended vistas. A tall red rose tapping at the window, tawny spread of sycamores reaching up to tug at first clouds, green of morning rolling onto the lawn, familiar sounds of family waking, a blessing on the day.

These are the gifts I bring you, hands cupped with all my small victories, my tiny moments, my little treasures, with the wish that they may somehow garland one brief moment for you in this season of remembrance.

For remembering is the nicest gift of all. As the years trudge along in unending procession, memory can trot back and forth like an eager puppy, tail-a-wag, visiting here and visiting there. And, as I take one day each year to write to you, to find my grassy knoll and let the world simply turn under me, I realize how many paths we've walked, what vistas we've seen and what marvelous friends have been beside us. Like kites being called by vagrant winds, we have been pulled this way and that and yet, always, we have been anchored to reality by the silken cord of family. One of two of us go away for awhile, to school, to work, for pleasure and like water flowing into a furrow, the rest of us fill in the empty places. This is the pattern now as our young adults move out and into their own paths. But, always, there are those sweet moments when we catch up to each other and go side by side or, best of all, the whole troupe together.

And this year our journeyings have taken us many places. To bayous embroidered with waterlilies in east Texas, and to make new friends who speak with silken sounds and slow mouths. To golden summered Cotswold country in England with vibrant gardens rimming stone cottages. To lovely old London, as tawdry and as tantalizing as ever. To Boston in the bit of clearest cold and across our desert mesa lands with sky an overturned turquoise bowl above our heads. Cities and villages and all those haunting empty places between, we've brought them all home again with us this year.

Elmo and Stacy are finishing *The Saga of Soggy Bottom* and planning new films. Jody is completing her last semester at Santa Monica College and looking forward to exciting new educational challenges. Toby is at a still point in his life and waiting for a new beginning. And I am here, as always, in the kitchen, the heart of our home and, I hope, the heart of our family.

Outside the bright sun denies that it is Christmas come again. Hummingbirds still stitch the garden hours and more flowers are a-bloom than ought to be. But in the cellar the old Santa dolls have grown impatient. Stacy's wooden flute lies on the piano bench. Poinsettias are tipping red and the air is getting nippy. The first of your cards and letters have arrived and wait to be ribboned to the stair railings. There is a whisper in the sky akin to that before the first rain comes. Leaves float slowly down to lie like small brown barques upon the ground. Cats move into rocking chairs and the dog moves closer to the fire. Night comes home earlier and morning keeps her keeps her hair pinned up with pale stars longer. And now that I have written you, I feel the ripeness of the year. It says another chapter has been lived and I must count again the many memories the year has brought before I add them to the beloved jumble already stored away.

My ears are waiting to listen for the cascade of Jody's laughter and Elmo's teasing voice. I yearn to hug Toby and find Stacy at the piano in the dim of early evening. The thoughts of lights and warmth and food a-waiting and those I love coming home fill me with all the eagerness of a child again.

Soon there will be a new year and new journeyings and new ventures and the heart lift of anticipation. But now there is the pausing and that pausing is more precious because time for it is so rare. I am loathe to leave it, and you, and pick up the busyness again.

So, before I do, let me send again those tender thoughts that are tissued away most of the year and bring smiles to wear as talismans against the chills of life and then let me fling open, once again, the doors to our home and to our hearts to wish you and yours the best of all good things.

Love,

Lorraine

Christmas, 1981

Dear Ones All,

Last night the winds blew summer down the street. And, while she hunts her chrysanthemum skirts and tugs a lemon sunshine shawl across her shoulders, it is time again to write to all of you. The birds have come from places where winter shouts with trumpet blasts to shelter in our garden. Hummingbirds flash electric green and blue between red blossoms, while the emperor of them all sits on the tallest twig of the towering avocado tree and sends out invitations. Velvet doves promenade through the rose garden to enjoy the sunflower seeds that rowdy bluejays have spilled out of the feeder. Lashings of linnets and swoopings of swallows bounce on the long branches of honeysuckle and blackbirds in bunches pepper the palm tree. Wild canaries with buttercup breasts dip in and out of the date tree to sample next year's harvest, and now and then I catch a glimpse of oriole like a golden arc against a darkening sky.

Outside my window there is a bush whose leaves are great green hands holding up the sky and, just now, it is crowned with plumes of blossoms that look like swags of ivory beads. The bees have found its bounty, and it is drenched and a-drone with their song. And, as if to put a shimmer on this writing, two monarch butterflies are fluttering through it like living cloisonné.

Each season shares its small miracles but this one most of all. The squirrels, whom I seldom see in summer, come down from the sycamores, which are dropping their leaves like bronze stars upon the lawn. And even after they have made their way around the perimeter of the garden wall, I still feel squirrel squiggles writing autumn poems. Our days are caught up in languor and the nights are apple crisp. And we know it is winter when the gulls bring the fog in from the sea in silken streamers.

This old house is content and so are we. This spring we gentled it, inside and out, by painting it a color which reminds us of apricots and cream. Then Elmo moved the furniture around so that mirrors wink at us from new places and the old wooden saints look solemn in different directions. Our collections have collected themselves in new rooms, but so comfortably that it is like seeing a dear face from another side.

So things are different but the same. Stacy has moved out and Toby has moved back in. She has taken an apartment in the same building where Jody lives and decorated it with her ethnic flutes, her Japanese prints and antique teapots and Daumier plates. Jody lives downstairs and Stacy lives upstairs, so they visit back and forth sharing cups of tea and sister talks, while Jody's kittens romp back and forth. Now that Toby is back with us the upstairs floorboards bounce again to his music and meaningful tread. They say you miss the patter of little footsteps, but no one will ever know how much I missed the cascade of big ones.

Soon we shall go down to the cellar and bring up Christmas. Already I imagine that I hear mutterings and small thumps from the big wooden box where all my old Santa dolls reside. We shall garland the hall and string the lights and open the big front door wide early this year because we shall be going to southern Oregon to spend Christmas week.

For Elmo has found us another home, one we hope to go to when he retires in two or three years. It is a small grey house looking out across a grand curving shore to the boulder and driftwood-bedecked ocean. There are pine and redwood rainforests not far behind, and a tang to the air, a richness to the earth that beckons to us. We know that one day we shall have to push out walls and raise ceilings to encompass at least part of all we have garnered in forty years of marriage. But, for now, the house will wait and we will fill its corners with our laughter and light our Christmas fires upon its hearth and share, the five of us, yet another rooftree. As small children, our three used to ask me each time we set out to a new country, "Is this another Dad-venture?" It was and, again, always will be.

Their careers will undoubtedly keep them here between the many visits we hope for, because each is embarked in a different direction. Stacy's comprehension and creativity in the film industry has made her invaluable as Elmo's partner. Toby is growing with a new company which manufactures telephones for the hearing impaired and is considering resuming his education next spring. Jody is commendably into her third year of college and the first of intensive nurse's training.

They are handsome and charming young people and Elmo and I are delighted to have them as friends and companions. Stacy's new ambience has only added to the distinctive aura she has always created and what is remarkable to me is that the heavier the responsibilities, the lighter her heart grows. Toby is finding the steadiness he searched for so long, but without any dimming of the buoyancy of his personality. Our Jody continues to grow more beautiful as she both radiates and reflects the joy she gives to others. If ever there was a double rainbow, it is Jody.

As for Elmo, what can I say? What praises are there that I haven't told? Each year he grows in every direction. He leads and we follow. He astounds us with his talents, delights us with his enthusiasms and is the polestar of our compass.

Now, having started this letter by finding small miracles, I discover I have found big ones. With a family like mine and with friends like you, I am truly blessed. And so, in this joyous season as in all seasons, I celebrate you, dear ones, one and all.

May you each, in this time of holy days and holidays, find your blessings commensurate.

With much love,
Lorraine

Christmas 1982

Dear Ones All,

Last night winter sounded a trumpet call of wind and came slashing in off the ocean. Summer, who had been clinging to the year with golden tipped fingers, has gone.

All night long rain beat against the house, shoving under the sills, sluicing off the roof, racing down the walks until our street became a river strewn with paisley eddies of golden leaves. Doors and windows ignored their latches and slammed open, slammed shut. Elmo and I were up in the grey darkness holding fast against the battering. By early morning, soaked and exhausted, we were somehow strangely exhilarated keeping our home secure, once more, against a storm.

So soiled curtains are being laundered, fans are drying sodden carpets, puddles have been mopped up and fur and feathered creatures comforted. I've put out seed for sparrows and linnets, sunflower kernels for doves and jays and laughed to see tiny, determined hummingbirds helicopter around their hanging bottle of nectar as it circles in the wind. The new dog, Coco, who galloped around with us in the night, has jumped back into her sleeping box and tucked nose into tummy. The old dog, Fawn, long ago sneaked into bed and under the covers with Toby. The cat, after one glance out the window, curled up in the laundry basket. Only our resident squirrel remains tucked up somewhere under the eaves.

Elmo left for work reassured that I can cope with the cleanup after we shared a pot of coffee with the emergency crews repairing downed cables and fallen trees. Suddenly bright sun is dancing atop fast scudding clouds while trees, like ruffled green umbrellas, bobble and bend against straggling gusts. Roofs all around are steaming over a fresh-washed world and I am happy.

Yesterday my house was shiny clean from front to back and top to bottom and the garden groomed and tidy. But that was before nature stomped in and shook things up! Yesterday I was complacent. Today I am humbled. But isn't that how it should be, sometimes, when we take sunshine and satisfaction for granted?

Now, looking back over the year, I can only remember the fine times, the fun times, the frantic times forgotten. And a family as busy as ours always has a plentitude of both.

In March we gained a grand new business family with the merger of the Gaylord and Yongestreet companies. I was given the exciting job of decorating their new offices and getting everyone in and settled in two weeks. But, thanks to wonderful workers and the enthusiasm of everyone involved, it worked like a charm. And the creative energies and compatibility generated still continues unabated in both the motion picture and television departments.

After completing the delightful *Soggy Bottom, U.S.A.*, Elmo embarked on filming the tender story of *Man, Woman and Child*. Production here gave us the chance to meet and work with new friends and then go to France for a ten-day reunion with companions and a country we dearly love. Stacy is just completing *Volvere*, a Spanish language film, produced in Mexico. Both of them are engrossed in planning more exciting projects as the company grows and prospers. *Hee Haw* continues to rollick along with a new season of episodes completed and the television division is also successfully involved in the *Glenn Campbell Show*.

Our comings and goings have been many, but seeing many of you in Arizona, Oregon, Nevada, Nebraska, South Dakota, Wyoming and New York as well as far away France, England, Italy, and Norway has made it all worthwhile.

A wistful Jody has driven us to and from the airport many times but her travel time will come next year after she completes her R.N. degree and Certification. Dedication to college and job has kept her pinned down physically but her blithe spirit still soars, matched only by our pride and the joy she gives us with her enchanting personality.

Toby is about to embark in two directions at once: a new job and enrollment in intensive computer training. Today he is bouncing all over the house anticipating the bright new horizons and opportunities ahead.

No wonder, then, that we all cherish our times together, to hug, to laugh and be silly, to catch up with everyone's latest news. That's why this holiday season will mean so much to us, more, perhaps than in years past when it was just the natural, sweet ending to an easy year. Like the aftermath of last nights' storm, this demanding and difficult year deserves a very special culmination.

So, as soon as I finish this letter to you, I shall move on to the joyous tasks of Christmas. I will put Mozart on the record player, spill cookie cutters onto the counter, sit the old Santa dolls on the steps, admire the way Toby has strung the colored lights, hold my finger on the ribbon while Elmo ties bows on his packages and find the carols for Stacy and Jody when they come over carrying their wooden recorders. A glow of contentment will spill over the confusion. I will be caught up with the welcoming and wonderment of all the good things in my life. And I will hope, as always, that you will be rich in love with me as I am rich in the loving friendship you have given through the many, many years,

Love,
Lorraine

Christmas 1983

Dear Ones All,

When I was a child, paper and pencils were precious. Each new school term, my grandmother bought me a yellow five-cent pencil to last and be taken care of. Sharpened with a paring knife, buttoned into my school bag, it was somehow symbolic, the talisman of learning. But, by and by, as lessons and homework wore it down, as sums and vocabulary were practiced on any and all hoarded bits of paper—leftover envelopes, backs of old letters, even the margins of newspapers—my shiny new pencil, now pockmarked by reflective toothmarks, diminished into a well-worn stub. But even then it was special, as special as a fresh unsullied piece of paper, reserved always in our family for important things like poems, thank-yous and love letters. That long ago parade of pencils, worn down to less than a penny's worth, became one of childhood's best remembered toys for by cutting a circle out of cardboard and coloring a design on it and fitting it halfway down the pencil stub, it became a top. And, oh, the hours I spent twirling and observing the designs wheeling and blurring and changing into new and gaudy patterns. My mind flew with the kaleidoscopes of color and movement even as Grandma's ingenuity had taught me the means to indulge in fantasy as well as to deal with facts.

Today, a glance at shoebox brimming full of leftover pencils took me back, not only to the beginnings of communication, but to the many letters sent and received along the flowing years. And that golden chain of leavings without letting go, those glad reachings out to touch and be touched again made me rejoice while I hurried through my morning chores. I gave each dog a succulent bone and saw them settle, content, on the lawn, brushed Puddy cat black satin smooth, poured ruby juice into the hummingbird feeder, filled the seedbox for the jays and linnets, the resident sparrows, and seldom-glimpsed orioles. I even cut bread cubes to wedge into the crotch of the tree not ten feet from the window where I sit writing for the impudent, scolding squirrel who often watches me.

Then I left the sun hopscotching over the drifting sycamore leaves and the autumn-tainted breeze ruffling the chrysanthemums to be with all of you again, to share some of the joys of another year that has spun past as busy, as gaily, as the turnings of my childhood tops.

We've worked hard as we always do but, for us, our work has always been joyous for it is done in collaboration with creative and caring people. No matter that there are disappointments and crises and a heavier-than-ought-to-be-load, there are always good companions from the past and each new venture, each new voyage, brings us more.

This New Year found Elmo and me in New Mexico but hurrying home to be with Stacy, Toby and Jody. In January Toby enrolled in an intensive computer training course which he finished with skill and alacrity by October. Meanwhile, Jody was intently immersed in her last term of college and by July she had graduated with honors as a registered nurse and had passed her state board exams. Stacy was off to Europe in February to set up and oversee production on the film *To Catch a King*. In March, Elmo, after supervising the premieres of *Man, Woman and Child*, was off to London to co-produce the stage musical of *Marilyn*.

In April he celebrated—can you believe it?—fifty years in the motion picture industry and was honored by so many of you who have worked with him. And then, for his 70th birthday, he took me and his sisters and his brother and sister-in-law on a marvelous two-week trek to Tennessee, the beautiful state where the Williams branch of the family originated. Then, in September, we shared a California reunion with Elmo's mother's side of the family to celebrate the Vaden's fiftieth wedding anniversary.

By October, Stacy had finished her back and forth to Europe journeys for the film and so, to relax, she invited me to go back with her again. We spent two delightful weeks in Greece, climbing stony, bee-busy mountains, walking along the sea, filling our curious minds with the beauty of ruins and archeological excavations, driving to sun-drenched villages, stopping to take photographs. Then we flew for brief visits with dear friends in Munich, Paris and London who spoiled us with such loving attentions that we never wanted to leave. But, then, there was home waiting and Elmo's open arms, and Toby's bearhugs, and Jody's laughing eyes to call us back.

So here we all are together again, the spinning tops at rest but just for the while. Jody and Toby are questing for career opportunities. Elmo and Stacy are putting together new projects. And I am, like the pencil stub, trying to provide a center point of stability for them all.

We will be in Oregon and the little seafront home we purchased two years ago for the Christmas holidays. It will be a time for long walks along the driftwood decorated sands, for vistas of storms moving across tossing seas, for brilliant sunrises over fishing boats waddling like strings of ducks out to sea, for the scent of fresh cut pine and the warmth of roaring fires but, most of all, for the blessing of time to just be together.

And, as always, there will be time for remembering all of you and rejoicing in the love of families and the gifts of friendships. Our love will go curling with the woodsmoke up the chimney and drift with the winds to wherever you are, bringing much more than my words on this piece of paper can express—so much more—gratitude and joy that you are you and that you belong to us, and that we can greet you again...and pray God's love upon us all.

Love,
Lorraine

In 1984, Lorraine's college named her Woman of the Year. She had graduated in 1939—the only protestant at Immaculate Heart. She loved the nuns that were her teachers and kept contact with them through the years that followed. The articles she wrote yearly for the alumnae paper about her travels were collected and read to those still attending the college. Ten years from the day Lorraine was honored, Immaculate Heart closed its doors for the last time. Sadly, Lorraine sat down to pen her remembrances. Her letter is a departure from the others in this collection, but it has been included in praise of all teachers everywhere.

– Elmo

1984

Immaculate Heart

As a girl, which surprisingly enough, I once was, I used to sit on that yellow fireplug just up the hill a little way behind us. I liked being there, especially after classes, in the last glow of sunset when the first pinpricks of lights sparkled across the city.

From there I could look out over the campus and then over Hollywood, and beyond that to the sea, and beyond that (I thought) to the rest of that vast, waiting world.

And, sitting up there, I sang. IHC was a school full of singers in those days. It didn't matter if you eventually ended up a biochemist, or a social worker, or even a Mack truckdriver. At IHC you were *also* a singer.

And *such* songs we sang! Words and melodies spilling happiness out from this hillside, like gulls finding the wind currents, like minnows darting across a pond. And, funnily enough, it comforts me now to think those words, those melodies, are out there still, drifting through the galaxies.

But, then, there were other words here at IHC. Words not sent cartwheeling out, but kept here. Words given back and forth between two people, conversations. Words spoken by one person to a group—education.

Words committed to paper. Words proclaimed bravely from onstage or whispered in chapel. Shouts and laughter echoing in the halls, going uphill and down, glowing through the trees, winding along the paths. Today we call them memories. And today we have tried to gather back a few words—a very few—to tell you, our teachers, how we feel about you. And, do you know, there aren't enough words bright enough nor right enough.

You were our friends, you befriended us. You were our counselors and you counseled us. GIVERS you were, and how generously you gave! You gave us an oasis between childhood and maturity with beautiful buildings and lovely gardens, and a style and grace to live among them.

You gave us classes that melded us into a community of students. And yet you *called out* our individuality so that we would never be faceless in any crowd.

You gave us discipline so that *whatever* challenges lay out there beyond the campus, beyond Hollywood or even beyond *beyond*...we could meet them capably and with courage.

You were *all* these things, and more too. But, most of all, you were teachers.

You taught us a lot more than the college catalogue promised. You taught us what was *beyond* the page as well as what was on it...that good writing was as important for a love letter as it was for a doctoral thesis...that a devils-food cake was a chemical formula just as surely as the most complicated vaccine...that the principles of social relationships were just as useful in potty training a two-year-old as they were in running a corporate structure.

You taught us to do more than look; you taught us to see. You taught us to do more than listen; you taught us to hear. And you taught us to do more than *merely accept life;* you taught us to *reflect it back*—and shine!

You taught us, by example, to be humble in positions of power and yet to take pride in humble tasks.

You taught us to be gentle, most times, yet you taught us too that anger was permissible as long as it was clean and sharp and scraped away the rough edges of frustration and resentment. *Yes*, it was from *you* that we learned to give way to the little things, but to stand firm, to stand fierce if necessary, against the big things.

But, of all the things you taught us, perhaps the most important is this: that the best way, perhaps the *only way,* to say thank you for what you have been taught is to teach it to others! And that lesson I think we have learned.

For what you taught to us on this lovely hill has flowed out like drifts of mustard weed across the barren hills. And, as those *we* have taught will eventually teach *others*, it will never cease to flourish, to multiply, and to magnify.

Now, on this difficult day when we know our beloved college must close, when tears tend to roll, when it is hard to speak around the lump in our throats, you must teach us again!

To be asked to celebrate what is to all of us, to each of us, a terrible blow is but a headshake away from impossible.

So, you see, we still need you to carry us forward with the same faith, the same fruitfulness, with which you taught in the past.

That way, with your guidance, we can continue to find the tomorrows as we have found the yesterdays, filled with a joy so pervasive that it will well up and wash away the hurting.

Help us to know that there is a togetherness, a sense of family, that neither time nor circumstances can eradicate, and that the spirit of Immaculate Heart College will continue to bless us all.

Thus, it is in that hope, in that belief that we salute you, we honor you and we love you.

For all that you are, from all that we are, we thank you.

Lorraine

Christmas, 1984

Dear Ones all,

Our garden has two magnolia trees. One has flourished since this house was built more than fifty years ago and, this morning, stands like a giant green candelabrum lifting slender white buds to a dove-grey sky. It is part of the heritage of this lovely old home. The other magnolia tree I planted soon after we moved here, a mere twig with only eight leaves and two tiny almond-shaped buds. Elmo laughed and called it my knee-high tree. The first winter, to my chagrin, all the leaves fell off but, then, when spring came, those tiny buds swelled and puffed out and burst open into magnificent rose-mauve blossoms with hearts of gold. I was vindicated, so much so that now my knee-high tree has stretched tall enough to trellis the upstairs windows. It reminds me that every dreary winter is followed by a redeeming spring.

It tells me, too, of the growing years we've known in this home, of the gatherings together of family and friends, of laughter and love that entered and stayed. The rooms are crowded with happiness, our fires burn bright and contentment sits beside us. But this is a home meant for a big family and now that our three are no longer knee-high but grown tall enough to search out their own dreams, it is time for Elmo and me to make yet another home, to plant yet another garden.

We have discovered just the place, a lovely promontory of land in southern Oregon, curving out into the ocean, beckoning sun and wind, presenting unending vistas of surf and sand and rocky shores. A talented young architect is already drawing plans for a home and Elmo and I are as eager to bring it to fulfillment as two pups tugging on a slipper. Oh yes, it will be hard to leave! Already our eyes have glinted with tears at the mere thought and we distribute sighs and remember-whens whenever gentle nostalgia taps us on the shoulder. But this home will stand, like the grand old magnolia tree, and shelter another family. And we, like the young tree, will find a new spot to put down roots and reach up and out to new friends, new enchantments.

Early next year, Elmo and I will go to spend some months in our little ocean front home in Oregon. He has but recently returned from painting it and putting down new carpeting and moving in the first pieces of furniture and some of the lovely bits-and-pieces we have collected from so many places. His enthusiasm for that dramatic windswept promontory is so contagious that it cannot help but alleviate the pangs we feel at the thought of leaving this house. It will be a place for Stacy and Toby and Jody to visit and vacation with us, to take long walks along the rocky beaches, to watch sun and clouds sweeping southwards, to meet with gulls and pelicans and minnows in tide pools, and to sit beside us around the driftwood fires and fill yet another home with togetherness.

Officially, I guess, Elmo has retired but, so far, he has been busier than ever. Even so, like a child once told me, at least he has time for more "want-tos" and not so many "have-tos". He has just finished a lighthearted film with young friends in Tennessee and is trying his best to resist all the other tempting offers coming his way. It seems that when folks find a good man, they never want to let go. I concur! Still the opportunity to paint and garden and play golf and sort through our accumulation of memorabilia should give him a welcome respite from the rigors of film making and fill at least some of the nooks and crannies of his every-questing temperament.

Stacy continues with the Gaylord organization and has just completed production on a series of twenty-six films for television titled *Explore*. Her many talents and creative acumen are just as bright and broad as that radiant smile she flashes. Professionally she manages to combine all that was splendid in the entertainment industry with all the exciting new things yet to come. Europe still calls to her and friends there urge her to join them in their projects, but it looks as if she will stay on this side of the ocean at least a little longer.

Toby has become domesticated. With a charming girl friend and his own apartment, he luxuriates in his quiet, settled routine after busy days spent as head of a computer department for a manufacturing firm. For the first time he knows the satisfactions that accrue from independent accomplishments and has set his sights high and is working hard to reach his goals. Whenever he can, he stops by our house, bringing in a burst of conversation and a big Toby hug. What delights me is that, even though he is away from home, he is somehow closer than ever.

Jody has had an enormous responsibility and challenge this first year in her position as an R.N. With dedication and exceeding compassion, she has done a truly remarkable job even though the very intensity of her caring has taken a toll on her time and energy. Her work and sharing with all her friends who are also starting out on new careers keeps her more than busy, but when we are together it is as it always was with Jody, like sunshine sparkling through the rain.

Once I wrote you that as much as we hated to see our children grow up, we could hardly wait to meet them as adults. They have grown up. We have met them. They are wonderful.

So, with greetings from the grown-ups, Stacy, Toby and Jody, the perpetual un-grown-ups, Elmo and Lorraine, send you best wishes for the joys of this holiday season. May your new year be knee-high with opportunities and may it surprise you with both expected and unexpected beauty. Remember, too, that whatever the sky overhead, storm on one horizon and sunshine on the other, it always stretches far enough and wide enough and high enough to cover us all. It keeps us close in thoughts and ever grateful for having one another.

With much love,
Lorraine

California, 1985

Dear Ones All,

For the Williams tribe of almost-gypsies to stay for fifteen years in one home is remarkable. We almost feel as if our feet are rooted in the garden and our hearts painted on every wall, as if each stairpost and doorsill grew out of us. Still, when you take down a painting from where it has hung for a long time, it leaves its outline on the wall. And so we hope it will be with this old house. It was desolate and unhappy when we came and we gave it back its beauty and filled it with love. So, for whatever other families come here to live, I like to think that our shadows will stay on the walls and our joys remain to bless it.

Perhaps Oregon will only be our summer home and we shall find a smaller home here as well. After all, heartstrings can only stretch so far! And Elmo has many calls upon his time and his wisdom and the one thing he has never learned to say is "no". But whatever comes I know it will be good because it always has been good. So changes ahead for us glint like the sun just slipping past sunlit hills into the sea. It brightens the sky and then darkens it and then brightens it again. Clouds glow from flame to muted rose to lavender grey. You cannot help but watch it in fascination, wondering what comes next. So, regardless of what comes next in life, we wait for it also, sometimes with reluctance, sometimes with anticipation or perhaps with a blend of both.

Elmo and I agree that it is lovely to bask in the autumn years, to be free to do those things we want to do, to go those places we want to be. And what a joy to watch at the same time, our three young people moving into the bright summertimes of their lives. Stacy has been Executive in Charge of Production for three fine films this year. Jody has now found a less exhausting but equally rewarding nursing position and Toby is casting about for a computer programming assignment worthy of his talents. There are changes ahead for them as well, but they have learned to face them with a measure of optimism learned, I hope, from us.

It changes. It changes. And, again, it stays the same. And that is how it should be. How lucky we are to be able to recall the past with such a sweep of sentiment. How fortunate to share the present with family and friends we cherish. How exciting to look ahead to all the good things that are waiting.

This is Christmas, then, another time, and for all it means to us we give thanks. We hope its joyous reflections reach out to you and yours to let you know how very much we value the gift of your friendship and your love. It is returned many times over and beribboned with the fervent wish that, for all of us, the afterglow will linger through the year ahead.

Love,
Lorraine

Christmas, 1986

Dear Ones All,

I hurried down the cellar steps to rummage amidst our accumulations of forty-six years for some long forgotten item. The instant I picked up that old tin box of marbles and heard the rattle clatter, my childhood was standing there beside me. I was again eight years old, sitting on my parents' front porch, playing jacks with Mary Ann and Patty but watching with envious, sidelong glances Billy and Tommy and Eddie playing marbles. You see, in those days, marbles were for boys and "boistering".

The marbles in the old tin box I have found in many places, mostly unexpected, but garnered for Elmo. You see, he can call them by names like aggies or clearies or pig shooters and still can hunker down and try to teach the rest of us to knuckle them out of a circle. To no avail though, for none of us could grow up with Elmo except as he now takes us back to his boyhood through storytelling.

But how wonderful to be able to go back to yesterday places, to catch what-was like falling leaves, listen to voices that have moved on to eternity, to cup our hands around those moments that somehow made us what we are.

This is the time of year for memories. It is the coming quiet of winter blown in on crisp winds that send clouds chasing after vanished summer. It is wisps of wood smoke and tangles of lingering chrysanthemums. It is a hush before the carols play. It is a foot pause before stepping into the holidays. For me, it is being with you just for this little while.

Each year this Christmas letter is my gift to me, a task I come to with trepidation lest I falter in conveying how much each of you means to me, a search for ways to say the same things in yet another way. As I talk of comings and goings, of growing-ups and growing-outs, just ordinary things, I want so much to share the small triumphs and jubilations that make them extraordinary to me.

Every year goes by so quickly. Every year is like a puppy chasing its tail, round and round, with pure delight in the chasing. And, by the time one game is ended, it is time for the next one. Each has its victories and its losses, its joys and sorrows, its alones and togethers, which, when we add them all up, we call our lives.

Many of the things I told you last year, I shall tell you again this year. Elmo has officially retired but Elmo is working just as hard as ever. Whenever someone who needs him calls upon his many talents, he is there for them. But, between times, he revels in a golf game, or finds ways to make this old house and garden even lovelier while still managing to get us, from time to time, to southern Oregon to ponder and plan the home we hope to build there next year. He has just finished a film he made in Tennessee with Stacy and other good friends and is spending long days in the cutting rooms. But soon he will be free again to return to the house plans and try to find room for all the treasures we have hugged home from our many moves.

Stacy has had a most productive and exciting year. Two of the films she made were nominated for Emmy Awards and she has also received a number of awards for her own dedication and fine cinematic abilities. She has bought a small but charming home, a condominium, which I find to be as serene, pristine, and quietly elegant as Stacy herself.

Toby has plunged exuberantly into a new position as Assistant to the Director of Operations Services for a prominent marketing concern. He has even moved to an apartment two blocks from his work so he can start earlier and stay later to find solutions to the many challenges that computers seem to convey.

Jody, too, is making marvelous progress in her nursing career. An intensive course in Spanish has given her the ability to dispense the special kind of care and caring that she has always given in two languages now. Her great joy this year has been a first brand new car, one almost as beautiful as she is.

But for all our happy times, we have known sad ones too. Our wonderful sister-in-law, Johnnie, has left us and we have also lost Evelyn and Corita, such splendid friends. Now we strive to find comfort in words that Corita once gave us: "She whom we love and lose is no longer where she was before. She is now wherever we are." In memories, memories, and all of them good.

Already I can feel the quiet of now giving way. A glance out the window shows evening moving in, settling over golden hills and a grey-blue sea. Sunset is rouging the sky before the first stars can appear. This year, too, calls out in its persistence and patterns. Time to make ready for Christmas. Time to repeat traditions and replenish the spirit. Time to fling open the doors and our hearts for all who come to find us here.

We shall, as always, look forward to hearing from you. And we shall, as always, enclose another year of gratitude and love, of memories in the little boxes of our hearts, just for you. Be very much blessed!

Love,
Lorraine

Christmas 1987

Dear Ones,

It has been a capricious year! All last night the winds shook the towering old sycamore trees like gypsy tambourines. Leaves rocketed over the roof and tumbled into swags of the bougainvillea and filled the round pond until it looked like it was topped with crisp meringue. I huddled under the down comforter and Coco stayed curled into a brown ball in the shelter of her doghouse. But this morning the sky was an innocent blue, the pale sun was as warm as melted butter and I had work to do. Elmo would be home in a few days and I wanted house and garden ready to welcome him.

I put on my garden clothes, gathered rakes and brooms and trash containers and got busy unbuttoning leaves from the tall hedges and scooping them from around the ankles of the bushes. I edged my way between the tiny plants tucked in for spring and tossed armful after armful of crackling tan onto the green of grass. I swooshed leaves out from under cars and up over the curb until, at long labor's last, I had a mountain of leaves in the center of the lawn. I straightened up just long enough to admire what I had accomplished when suddenly, as if a plumb line had dropped from the sky, a whirlwind hit! I was at the center of flying, soaring, spiraling leaves, a vortex that claimed my breath and sucked my spirit into an upward flight so unexpected that all else was for that moment obliterated. And, then, as if with a great sigh, it was silent, a silence so silent that it denied sound and then leaves came drifting calmly and peacefully down again. And there they lie now like a comet's tail come to rest.

Now I need to be with you so I have come inside to write this letter and reflect upon so many things you have, even without knowing it, shared with me. With Elmo gone a great deal of the time supervising the building of our new home in Oregon, I have had the solitude for remembering, remembering of the kind that exists not only in the "thens" of time but touches both the "nows" and the "forevers" as well.

Before I leave this lovely old home, I need to pack more than barrels and boxes. I need to run my fingers along the railings that Stacy and I painted, moving bottoms and paint cans from step to step while conjugating irregular French verbs for schoolwork. I need to smile at the window pane, replaced when young Toby who, never having played baseball in Europe, discovered to his surprise that a softball wasn't that soft after all. I need to laugh again over the time when Elmo and I were gone and the nectarines were ripe and Jody made them into jars of golden jam and then labeled them peach because she couldn't spell nectarine. I need to see without seeing the beloved pets that shared our lives for the span of theirs: Tabatha sitting demure in the kitchen window with all her stripes matched and only her pink mouth askew, Homesteader, all wind-ruffled, mewing silently for his dinner, and Tarbaby, the clown cat, sleeping on his back front paws stretched out over his head, soaking up the sun as no sensible cat should. And there was tawny little Fawn dog, ears pricked up and brown eyes watching my every move through the glass door.

And wherever I go outside I cannot forget Elmo chasing us all around the house with the garden hose, precipitating one of those famous all-out water fights. Oh, my dears, there are so many good memories and not enough hours to gather them in so I shall have to take them with me. And I will.

But, while we are still here, I will pause often to hear your steps in the hall, your laughter around the table, and feel the joy of your coming and the welcome of your letters. Our kitchen will be crowded again with all of you, perched at the counter or leaning against the walls, conversations mingling with the fragrance of cooking and Christmas. It will be like the description I once wrote on a small scrap of paper when our small children told of the adventure of cooking a meal without grown people around: "Somebody peeled and another body sliced and then the last body cooked. But everybody ate!" Those few long ago words seem to encapsulate the sharing we have known so long and enjoyed so much.

I know our tree will sparkle brighter this year because of all the trees before it. And the fire will warm us with the presence of all who have ever gathered around it. And the hugs will be many and many more. Hugs for those who are here and hugs for those who are no longer here but who will always be near to us. For many that we have loved have left us this year, too many, too dear, too soon.

Yes, this has indeed been a capricious year. Our children now gone their grown-up ways have graduated from jobs to careers. They have had to learn that life entails disappointments and also inequities as well as achievements and rewards. There have been strong emotional upheavals to be resolved as they came to know that parents as well as children are vulnerable and not without flaws. There has been the truth of our eventual move always shadowing our steps and the need to turn this sanctuary home over to another family. It is hard to accept the distance that will lie between us for we have been close together for so much of our lives. Still there is the comfort of knowing that, no matter how far the ribbons of love must reach, we can always wind ourselves into each other again.

In Oregon Elmo and I will go to sleep to the beat of the sea and wake to the cry of the gulls. There will be a new garden to make and new friends waiting. The old furnishings will settle in against new walls but our windows will look out upon the same sunrises and sunsets that spread out to touch you as well. We shall have storms to watch as well as days of silken seas. It will be living as living must be and we will accept it all as it comes simply because it must come.

Twice in recent dawns the earth has shuddered beneath this old house and I woke to a recognition of how fragile a hold we have upon all we cherish. And today it was a whirlwind that sent me in to tell you how good it is to have you and how good it is to belong to you. And the telling should be told for, too often, until we are caught up for a breathless moment, we cannot know how precious is that silence when the leaves—and the love—drift down around us again.

Love,
Lorraine

Lorraine Williams

Christmas 1988

Dear Ones all...

On this crisp sunny morning here in Oregon, memory has wrapped itself around my shoulders and, from this lovely new home, I have gone visiting my many others.

The first one I remember was Grandmother's when I was just going-on-four and knee-high in the glory of her garden. Pink and scarlet satin poppies brushing my cheeks, dinner plate dahlias bobbing over my head, and a carpet of blue forget-me-nots and purple verbenas to dance upon. My big brother, going-on-twenty, had built a pergola over the driveway to support the rampaging pink roses that were waiting to cover it. And then, may he be forever blessed, he built a swing beneath it and there I spent many happy hours under drifting petals.

Oh, there have been many homes since then. Some as humble as the tin roofed ranch shack nestled into a crevice on the dry New Mexican prairie and others as elegant as the Lord Mayor's flat in London's Eaton Square. Each has given more than shelter for each has brought its own blessings and benefits.

Elmo and I had always dreamed of building our own home and once, years ago, we almost made it with construction due to start December 8th, 1941. But then the sad news of December 7th sent us all off to our wartime lives. But, in retrospect, we realize that had we built that house we should probably never have known all the others that our travels have provided.

I remember that when peace came back and after what seemed like endless labor refurbishing our first home, Elmo and I used to climb to the top of the huge Acacia tree in early evenings just so we could look down on all that we had accomplished.

Later there was our first flat in London, so high under the eaves that the central heating never reached it but the shivers were small price to pay for the views over Hyde Park Gardens.

On our return to our second California home, high above the sparkling city, we became a family and I rocked wee Stacy while an owl family sat, solemn, on a slender branch of Eucalyptus tree and nodded approval.

But it was in the students' quarter of Munich that she could first stand at the window and wait for me to finish the housework so that we could go walking in the Englischer Garten. That was just before we moved to the small country house in Pullach where Toby and Jody came to belong to us and where, on winter nights when the snow piled high, we could tuck all three little ones under the down comforter with us.

By the time they were ready for tricycles and sandboxes we were in Paris watching shafts of sunlight brighten the Bois de Boulogne. And for their first school years we were again in London with playmates that are still their friends, interrupted only by a never forgotten summer spent in Ireland where waterfalls watched our long treks around the lake and across the mystic hills.

Back in California again we finally came to the growing-up house and there, sheltered by towering sycamores, we shared the sense of belonging—really belonging—to a home. Filled with joy and companionship for seventeen years, we welcomed friends, and garnered the rewards of all our many years together. But at last, when our children were grown and gone, Elmo and I knew that it was time to build the home we had dreamed of for so long.

The last Christmas at Corsica Drive was a time overflowing with gratitude in rooms that echoed many voices, in a garden that had known many flowerings. We said goodbye to that house with a hug that embraced it all. For, even as families need homes so do homes need families, and now that old house has a splendid new family whose laughter will always be an encore to ours and whose happiness an extension of all that went before.

Today, on a granite cliff high above a capricious sea with vistas reaching to forever and beyond, we have come to rest. Our home is small enough for two but big enough to welcome all who come to it. It is filled with windows to watch the languid flight of pelicans all-in-row or cormorants plunging like black arrows into the frothing waves in search of silvered minnows. Our old furniture has settled in easily, majolica has found its shelves, mirrors glance at new walls and the same paintings greet us.

Early mornings find us walking a long curving beach while Coco dog runs scallops along the wave-wet sand. Evenings find us watching sunsets spilling color over skies piled high with feather bed clouds. We wake to gull cries and go to sleep to the melody of waves.

Yesterday we went to the woods, walked on earth as brown and soft as velvet, breathed air as pure as crystal and came home with arms full of pine and cedar and glistening red-berried holly. Today Elmo has been searching out the Christmas ornaments and the old Santa dolls who are anxious to have a peek at their new home. And while I have been writing this, he keeps coming in with the eager trot of a new pup to show me what other treasures he has found again.

It is time, dear ones, to make this house a Christmas house. Time to reach out as I have done so many years to every one of you who have gladdened my heart with the gift of your friendship and love. In so many countries, in so many homes, you have been with us! And you will be with us again this year even though you may be far away. Yes, when Stacy comes with her smile that beggars the sun, when Jody's brown eyes start dancing and Toby's laughter bounces off the walls, it will be Christmas and you will be here.

But, before then, I will take time to go to my special place in the swing that Elmo made and hung in front of the picture windows—so that I could swing and look out at the sky and the sea and remember. And while I am swinging, back to the days of childhood through the years to now and forward to the ones yet-to-be, I will remember all the good things in my life and ask God to bless all of you who have given them to me.

Our homes, after all, are more than buildings. They are the repositories for all we have lived and loved in them. So this year, from our home to yours, may joy and contentment be with you now and in bright new years to come.

Love,
Lorraine

Brookings, Oregon, Christmas, 1989

Dear Ones all,

That great Pacific ocean that lies just outside our windows seems to permeate our lives with its majesty and its moods. This summer it seemed to take a vacation, lolling under the bluest of skies, barely nudging the great rocks and spreading delicate lace-edged waves along the shores. The birds that colonize the cliffs and rocks sailed like kite tails in processions across the sky. The great whales swam north once again. And it was good.

In the autumn days we looked to the hills where redwoods and pines stood sentinel with wisps of clouds tucked like silk handkerchiefs in the pockets of the valleys and riverbeds. An otter pair, sinuous and silent, came for a visit, gliding up the back steps, wet noses nudging the glass in the French doors and then, curiosity satisfied, undulated off into the side garden and back to the sea. And it was good.

Now winter has us wrapped in its arms. The winged creatures are gone to sheltered coves, whales back to southern waters, and the sea has found its voice again. It tells of voyages from far away in its timeless urge to lift great waves and fling them against the shore, one after another, rising higher and higher with long feathers of foam blown back over their shoulders before they curl and crest and fall, their journey finished. And it is good.

For a while we thought the sun had abandoned us and gone to live behind leaden gray skies. Rain drummed thunder songs upon the roof while rivers raced to the harbor to find fishing boats bobbing, impatient at their moorings. Always persistent, the gulls huddled on our rooftop waiting for me to walk to the mailbox so I could feed them. Swirling down around me, the juveniles with plaintive cries and the elders with shrill greetings. And I knew that it was good.

Today the sun surprised us, found us again, good Old Shiney-face is back! The sea, having played its joke on us, is laughing, sending waves rollicking along the shore. Elmo and our new rambunctious golden Labrador pup have gone out to play. The cats, uncurled from long fireside sleeps, are treading wet grass with discovering steps. Spider webs spangled with raindrops decorate the garden and, even though the day is calling me outside, I am spending this part of it with you. And that too is good.

As I sit here at this amazing contraption called a computer, I cannot help but reflect upon the astounding changes that have occurred in our lives and in the world in general. What once seemed impossible is now matter of fact. In every area of our lives technology has shaken us up, hustled us up, and led us to go beyond what was with promises of what is yet to be.

But whenever I come across a letter in Grandma Etter's delicate scrawl or the recipe for my pumpkin pie pencil-copied by my Mother, I want to stop and step back lest I lose what had so much meaning then. Our children chide me that I still write letters and send them "snail mail" in blue envelopes with stamps on the front. Somehow that seems to bring me in closer touch than typing it on this monitor and pushing an e-mail button that says "send" so that whatever communication I had in mind has fled in a mini-second.

Elmo and I still build wood fires. We still cook in pots and pans. We still share washing dishes, side by side at the sink. We still have conversations with each other, with family and friends. We still dig in the earth and plant seeds and bulbs and flowers both at home and in the lovely three-acre garden Elmo created in our community's Azalea Park. When the mood strikes us we sing or whistle and say once again that the old tunes were the best tunes. And we tease each other and laugh a lot. At those times technology must step aside for what was and will always be good.

So now as I sit addressing this Christmas letter to you, it gives me these few, very special, minutes to visit with you again, to go back to that place and that time when we were together, to string another bead on the garland of memories. As always we send you our best wishes for whatever you need…for comfort in times of sorrow, for joy in times of gladness, for a kitten purring on your lap, a dog bouncing to greet you, friends upon your doorstep, family with open arms to hug you. All this and more, God's blessings for you, on this season in which we give thanks for each and every one of you. And that is best of all!

With Christmas love,
Lorraine

Christmas 1999

Dear Ones All,

Many, many years ago when I was but a small fretful child recovering from an illness, my grandmother sat long hours by my bed. I called her "Moremama" probably because she was always with me while my widowed mother went out to work. One day, to amuse me, she put her button basket on my bed and gave me a piece of kitchen string. Then, as, one by one, I chose a button to put on the string, she told me the story of where that button came from. One, I remember was from her wedding dress, another from her father's army jacket, but every button had a story of someone and some place and some time in the past.

Today, once again, I am stringing memories onto the golden thread of the past. For, as the year ends, there is some long latent, instinctual need to tally up the happenings of the past and tuck them gently in a corner of the heart. For a clean slate, another year, a bright beginning is waiting just ahead.

There is no ordinary year, each one is unique, and yet the one just ahead makes us catch our breaths. A new year—a new century—a new millennium!

To tally up all that has happened in our lives before that anticipated moment, when the clock ticks over into what lies ahead, is both a challenge and a privilege. For, as we each get busier and busier in the mundane and ordinary everydays of our lives, we should pause on the threshold of tomorrow to celebrate all the yesterdays.

I have read again all the Christmas letters past, almost fifty years of them, and lived again the times we were together, the labors we shared, the laughter and the love. What wonder I felt in finding new worlds and new friends. London's aroma of lemon soap and coal fires and rumbling red buses. Paris with three small children big-eyed at their first glimpse of the Christmas tree. Munich and Kirchberg with snow and sleds and carols sung around the woodstove's warmth. Then California with family, and now here in Oregon rejoicing in the remembering of it all.

I know that in spite of all the publicity and predictions, the night of the new year will be just as dark as all the other nights our world has known. Waves will roll unconcerned onto the shore. The gulls will sleep with their heads tucked under wings, the dog will turn around three times before she lies down and the cats will roll up like satin balls. Everywhere small children will still dream small children's dreams. And benevolent sky will watch over them all.

For we are so lucky to have found each other, to have loved each other and, now, to be able to go—together—into what lies ahead. The journey has been good. The future will be better. And for all that lies ahead, Elmo and I send you our greetings and best wishes for you are the treasures in our lives, strung, like the buttons of my childhood, on our heartstrings.

With enduring love,
Lorraine

Christmas 2000

Dear Ones,

Sweet summer stayed so long this year that autumn had to tiptoe in. But now she has slowly gilded the alder trees and gathered morning mists from off the sea. Winter is waiting we know and will come when waves and wind conspire to match the calendar. So we wait, patient as the mountains wait, warmed by gentle suns to gather the last dahlias and chrysanthemums tucked in corners of the garden.

In families, too, the great timepiece of our lives surprises us sometimes. Plans and routines on which we depend can be disrupted, suspended, and change can catch us unaware. And this year has been one in which we all have had to learn to accept and adapt to the unexpected.

In July Stacy fell and tore the Achilles tendon in her right ankle. Then, too soon after surgery and a heavy cast, she flew to Canada to produce a major stage production. But the travel and stress caused her to suffer a stroke and be hospitalized for a month before she could return to Oregon. Now we are all home again, here in our house beside the sea, participating in her recovery. Each day some new small achievement is cause for rejoicing. Her courage has been rewarded by a strong sense of commitment for the future to use her many talents and legal expertise for the benefit of others who are incapacitated. We should always remember that there are rainbows in life, as in nature, when a storm is over.

Jody, too, has had a difficult year with the loss of her mother-in-law and the illness of her father-in-law. As wife, mother and daughter, homemaker and nurse, she continues to be the support and comfort of all. Her indomitable loving spirit is still the sunshine in so many of our lives.

Toby continues to excel in his profession as computer expert. Even though a lot of his free time is devoted to improving his home, thinning trees and landscaping his hillside property, he often finds time to visit us. Needless to say, we invariably have a list of things for him to do—usually pertaining to some so-called miraculous but, often for us, baffling modern technology. He is definitely our Star Warrior of the Fixit Galaxy.

Elmo, if course, is Elmo! What else can I say to all who know him. His energy never flags. His humor flows forth with the same joyous abandon. His health, outside of the minor aches and pains of eighty-seven years of unceasing yet rewarding toil, is remarkably good. And he is, as always, the lodestar of our lives, the essence of continual goodness.

Together as family we have, in this year of unseasonable seasons, learned to accept what has happened and to realize that there is a flow to our lives too. It is as eternal, as compelling as that wondrous sense of timelessness that prompts the sea, the sky, and the good earth to share its treasures with us. We have discovered that happiness may be sometimes hidden like the violets, but at other times it can surprise us, like sun shining through the rain, washing away sadness and filling the world with brightness. It is always there, our timeless treasure and this year, as always, we would send full measure of it to you, our cherished family and friends.

Lorraine

Lorraine Williams

Christmas 2002

Dear Ones all,

Storm on one horizon; sunshine on the other.

This was the summer of raging fires that threatened to destroy the magnificent Oregon forests. Over a million acres were burned before valiant efforts of more than six thousand firefighters, some from as far away as Canada and Australia, brought the great fire under control. For weeks smoke billowed up from the mountains behind us, the sky was leaden and the sun when it was visible was a dark orange blur. Smoke lay over the ocean like a great gray blanket and over our hearts as well. At last, at long last, the winds slackened and the cool damp air from the ocean swept in and the devastation ended.

Storm on one horizon; sunshine on the other.

In our personal lives we also know them both. Thank God for memories, indestructible precious memories. Intangible but ever present they are the green sprouts of life rising from the darkness, the soft winds blowing away the emptiness, the warm sun comforting our hearts.

So we go on. Elmo and I, even more aware of the wonders we have known these many years, feel blessed by a life so rich with family and friends. Changes and challenges, places and times gone by, all lived with the grace and gusto that have infused our lives. The years unroll like those red ribbons we strung across the times we shared and that we shall never forget. With hearts full of gratitude we thank you for being you and keep you always in our thoughts.

We send you each and every one our Christmas greetings and wish for you a New Year filled with love and laughter and the best of your heart's desires.

Love,
Lorraine

Christmas 2003

Dear Ones All,

The sea has been busy this morning. The waves have come grumbling into shore under a steady rain. Rivers and creeks are running full, spilling into the froth tossed upon the sand. The golden sun the sea always waits for has stayed hidden behind the mountains while drifts of cloud lie tangled in the tops of the highest pine trees.

Living high above the edge of the sea, we have become so accustomed to its many moods that its pulse seems as familiar as our own heartbeats. We rejoice when it rejoices and reflects the sky with vivid colors of celebration. We also understand when it is angry and beats in vain against the forever cliffs or simply lies quietly exhausted as if seeking solace amidst the great rocks.

We, too, experience sea moods. This year has brought us great sadness with the deaths of our sister Willie and our son Toby. And too many dear friends have also left us. Yet we find our solace in all the good memories they left, legacies of love and laughter, to help us carry on. Like the waiting sea we know the sun will find us again and paint great banners of red and gold across the sky before it sinks beneath the horizon giving us a farewell green wink. Then waves will once more come rollicking ashore, like small boys chasing each other along the sand, wanting to be first to splash in the shallows and laugh as the water ebbs back across the pebbled edges.

We are grateful for good health, wonderful families, marvelous friends and our busy life in a small and caring community. So even though we are here and you are there, we are still together in the many fond remembrances to times we shared with you.

Like the waves, thoughts of you keep coming back to us and always…with love…

Elmo and Lorraine

Reflections

Lorraine Williams

Brookings, Oregon, 2004

"Merci"

We once spent Thanksgiving in an old farmhouse in France. The grey stone buildings had huddled there so long in the fierce winds off the North Sea that they had sunk down into the rocky earth. The people, too, had known many hardships. We ate in the kitchen, for every French family the heart of the home. A huge room—high ceilinged, heavy beamed—with a long trestle table and rude benches pulled up to it. The smoky, plastered walls had been whitewashed (how many hundred times one can only imagine) but only down to—or up to—a place at eye level where someone had painted in old-fashioned script and in bold black letters six inches high:

SI TU REMERCIE LE BON DIEU POUR TOUS LES CHOSES QU'IL TE DONNE, IL NE RESTERA PAS TEMPS DE TE PLEINDRE.

The words went around three walls. "Ah," said our young French friend, "You are reading Grandmama's poem. She wrote it there when she was a young bride."

Grandmama was sitting in her chair by the fire, a tiny, black-shawled little old lady well into her nineties, and totally blind for more than fifty years.

"She has had much sorrow in her life," said her great-grandson. "Her husband was a fisherman lost in a storm at sea. Three sons were killed in the Fourteen-Eighteen War and two daughters died in childbirth. Then the Boche again—this last war—she lost five grandsons. Her poem comforts her."

"But if she's blind she cannot see it!" "Ah, but she does not need to see it as long as she knows it is there." 'If you will thank God for all the things He has given you, there will not remain time to complain yourself.'"

"For Elmo"

First the bud
Tight-folded
Hardly daring to let sun and love
Coax her to open

Then at last, a rose
As she was meant to be
Full, fulfilling, and fulfilled.

Ah, but what is left
When petals fall?
I dare not think
That that is all.

No. The seed pod stays
Holding all that was
All that's yet to be.
My song, my loving you
Will linger through eternity.

Lorraine Williams

"Dear Man"

Dear Man,

Once upon a time there were two people who loved each other so much that it was hard for them to talk about it. So for more than twenty years they resorted to writing invisible love words between the lines on laundry lists or chinking up brick walls with a mixture of one-third cement, one-third sand, and one-third happiness. Clothes were hung on the line and the clean, sweet flap of a sheet dancing in sun and wind was equal to the clean, sweet flap a heart felt when your loved one walked around the corner. And sometimes sorting nails was sorting happiness too—this jar for contentment and that one for dreams. And how many giggles fell into the cornbread batter and how many worries over what was ahead went up the chimney with the log smoke? It is hard to say. The heart was never meant to be a bookkeeper. It even loses track of the lonely beats, the frightened thuds, the anguished pauses when your beloved is away and a telegram arrives or the phone rings in the middle of the night! Silly heart, it doesn't even remember the steady, sturdy heartbeats of the work and duty days, the nothing special days, the nine-to-six days.

Maybe we should banish the heart as the symbol of romance and designate the hands instead. To smooth the wrinkles out of a bedspread, a jacket, or a sleepy forehead, to turn the screwdriver, to grasp the steering wheel, or to hoist a laughing youngster to the ceiling. Or the eyes...those mirrors of shared laughs, and the "I'll-tell-you-later" looks or the ones that say "Hey, you aren't bad looking at all considering..." Considering what? Why, considering that twenty years can be a long, long time in our lives even though it seems no longer than the slow closing and opening of an eye. And yet we need only empty out our pockets to find they have been so full of wonderful things like cinnamon rolls and semicolons, spaghetti and fried eggs at three in the morning, strips of rugs to braid, shingles to nail, leaves to rake, suitcases to pack, bulbs to plant, houses to paint, scripts to read, floors to wax, cars to name, letters to write, bills to pay, trips to take, babies to hold, to adopt, to cherish, to fret over, to lose sleep over, to get cranky over, and it all adds up—these and a thousand million more bits and pieces—to the fact that wherever certain people go they can always see sunrise on one horizon and storm on the other.

And isn't it wonderful to have some of both and to know that while your wheel of life is turning another turns in tandem? Not always riding the exact same bump, but waiting while you roll up out of a chug hole on your side of the road, and ready to climb the next hill with you or roll down into the next green valley, or cross the river.

I still can't say these things I want to say so please refer to my latest laundry list. God bless you, my man Elmo.

Lorraine

"For Elmo" (2)

Look at my hands
holding so much
My hands were so empty
until filled by your touch

Look at my arms
reaching out wide
No longer hugged
close to my side

And look at my hair
that was hair that was all
Today my hair
is a waterfall

Look at my body
and I will look too
What can this body
offer to you
Let it be like the earth
hungry for seeds
Ripe to be planted
with all of your needs

Then look at tomorrow
'cause yesterday's gone
smoothed out of my forehead
by the fingers of dawn

And look at the girl that
God gave a shove
And turned her into
THE WOMAN YOU LOVE

Going From Here To There

Dear Ones,

Life is like a topographical map. From our vantage point, standing in the bottom of a canyon gazing upwards, it is filled with enormous mountains.

How easy if life were a flat and open prairie land, filled with sweet-smelling grass and spangled with wildflowers. How good it would be to stand at the beginning of a journey and be able to see the end of it. To travel from milepost to milepost and tarry at green oasis, to drink from brimming wells and always, to be able to see the enormous gates of the city ahead waiting to swing open for us when we arrive.

How we do dislike those mountains! We get so tired and so discouraged as we climb and stumble and slip and fall back in our struggles to reach a summit. How often we are tempted to just stay in a pleasant valley and listen to the murmur of the stream and hide under a canopy of leaves and wish we never had to go on. How many times we start the next step of our journey with grudging hearts. And when we fall and scrape our knee and when the sweat itches a torment down our back, and breathing is a stab in the side and our legs tremble and our head throbs—how we hate climbing.

Yet, we know that suddenly the vertical path will slack off to an even plateau, the cool breeze that blesses mountain tops will touch our cheek, and that we will be there. How good it is to stand and look back and say: I came from way back there. Isn't it good to be here! Then we turn and look ahead and somehow that mountain doesn't seem as high as this one and after a rest we shall be ready to plunge down into the valley again and rest for the next climb.

Each of us walks his own way, chooses his own path, sets his own pace. Sometimes we share the road with loved one or friend. Sometimes we walk in rich silence and wonderment at the beauty of everything around us, sometimes we strew the miles with foolishness and laughter and song. Some people we overtake and outdistance. Some people we lag behind. Sometimes we grow discouraged and quit. Sometimes we wander aimlessly and get lost. Sometimes we rush and leap and struggle and almost batter ourselves against obstacles so enormous and so eternal that we could never hope to conquer them. Some of us are happy. Some of us are not. Sometimes we complain and cry until you'd think every inch of the way was a mile. Other times we feel our spirit glad within us and race like children in a morning meadow.

We climb the mountains of willfulness. We slide down into the valleys of despair. We stop to pile rocks of prejudice across the trail. We wallow in the quicksands of self-pity. We sleep in the stupor of laziness. We shout the mouthings of pride to hear them bounce back hollow and magnified from the blank rock face of self. And we are afraid and lost. We are wishing all the time we could reach up and take Our Father's hand so He could lead us safely home.

Why do we go on? What is it that compels us? Why should life be a journey?

It is heaven we hunt for, you know. That is why we make this journey. None of us know quite what it will be but we only know we must try to reach it.

It is simply that all things that begin must end. When we are born, we begin. We have nothing to do with it, it just happens. Are we then just like a flower seed that germinates, grows, sprouts, blossoms, withers, and dies? Are we then just like an animal, conceived, borne, reproducing, and dying? Or is there some additive element to man?

Why do we try so hard—to get from here to there. Plants and animals live only in their natural habitat and pattern. Only man strives to get above it! We are not merely blind instinctual creatures and we know it. There is an awareness in every man of the ultimate value and the uniqueness of his own individual soul. He knows he began and that he will end. He knows there must be a reason for his beginning and his end. And he spends his lifetime searching for it. Every second our heart ticks off takes us further away from the beginning and brings us closer to the end. The thought of this is what frightens us so much. We are afraid we shan't find the answer—the why—before it is too late.

And yet we have the answer within us. That essential spark within us is divine. It is a fragment of God. He, Who put us here. From whence we came and to Whom we shall return. In His infinite wisdom He knew we would be afraid. A spark is such a small thing to light vast darkness! So He sent us a Pathfinder to walk ahead of us, to climb the mountains, to travel the valley of the shadow of death. We must never forget, in our troubles, that the Pathfinder walked part of that trail with blood dripping from His hands and from His feet and from His side. And He walked alone.

I think that as an example of mankind,Jesus was magnificent. If I could not believe he was divine I should still admire and love him. But I think that as Divinity He was ever more magnificent! To step down to our level, to gird himself in mortal humility, to bear imperfections, to suffer for us and with us, to show us the way was the ultimate love that any man, divine or mortal, could ever demonstrate.

He says, "You are but a tiny spark—I am the Holy Flame that consumes all doubt, that burns away the chaff, that refines coarse metal into purest gold. I am the sun and the moon and the stars. I am the way, the life, and the resurrection. I am the hope of the world."

"Take Our Hands"

Father, take our hands,
Guide us along the path
When we are afraid, give us Thy strength

When we stumble, lift us up
When we sorrow, comfort us
When we hunger, feed and refresh us
When we fail, forgive us.

We lift our hands and our hearts
In a selfless gesture of faith.
In that gesture we express our helplessness
Our humility and our loneliness.

Take our hands and hold them
Fill our hearts with faith
For it is faith we lack
It is faith we cannot buy, or build

We cannot demand it as our right
We cannot reason it into being
We cannot even define it.

It is Thy gift.
Thou, alone, can give it to us.
Our Father, give us faith
For without it we are lost.

Give us faith, we pray, that we
As little children, Thy children
Shall enter, our hand in Thine,
The kingdom of heaven.

On August 16th of 2004, Lorraine journeyed on to another world, leaving behind this collection of letters and her endless love for all of us. Although we traveled extensively in Europe and the Middle East, Lorraine always made friends--the long-lasting kind. She gave us faith – in God, in truth, and in ourselves. She had no need to preach us a sermon; she was our sermon. She didn't need to tell us to grow tall in our spirit; she was our measuring stick and we knew it. She gave us courage so that in our time of stress we might be as indomintable, as humble, and as impervious to any – and every – evil as she was. Lorraine gave us hope for she believed in us and the power of her believing was as encompassing, as surging, as ceaseless as the sea. She was a beautiful person in every way, so her continuing journey must also be a beautiful one. Her life was filled with beauty. With all my heart I loved her.

- Elmo